# THE GOAL OF POSITIVE LIVING SKILLS IS:

BETTER CHILDREN

BETTER LEARNERS

BETTER CLASSROOMS

BETTER PERFORMERS

BETTER PEOPLE

BETTER RELATIONSHIPS

BETTER SOCIETIES

A BETTER WORLD

# THE PATH TO MORE POSITIVE LIVING IS:

POSITIVE FOCUS

CONNECTED FOCUS

LOVE/EMPATHY/CARING

APPRECIATION

LESS STRESS

MORE RELAXATION

SIMPLE JOYS EVERY DAY

# POSITIVE LIVING SKILLS

## Joy and Focus
## for Everyone

# Terry Orlick, Ph.D.

GSPH

GENERAL STORE PUBLISHING HOUSE
499 O'Brien Road, Box 415
Renfrew, Ontario, Canada K7V 4A6
Telephone 1.613.432.7697 or 1.800.465.6072
www.gsph.com

ISBN 978-1-897508-23-7

Cover, design, formatting: Magdalene Carson
Printed by Custom Printers of Renfrew Ltd., Renfrew, Ontario
Printed and bound in Canada

Library and Archives Canada Cataloguing in Publication

Orlick, Terry, 1945-

    Positive living skills : joy and focus for everyone / Terry Orlick.

ISBN 978-1-897508-23-7

    1. Self-actualization (Psychology). 2. Happiness. I. Title.

BF637.S4O755 2010        158.1        C2010-905944-1

*I dedicate this book to every child, teenager, and adult*
*in the world who has ever dreamed of*
*a better way, a better life, a better world.*
*Our shared goal is for every child born into this world*
*to be given an opportunity to learn Positive Living Skills*
*that will free each of them to live*
*a higher quality of life—now and in the future.*
*This goal is within our stretched human potential.*

## STEPPING STONES

Isn't it strange that Princes and Kings
And clowns that caper in sawdust rings,
And just plain folks like you and me,
Are builders for Eternity?
To each is given a bag of tools,
A shapeless mass and a book of rules,
And each must make ere life is flown,
A stumbling block, or stepping stones.

*—Author Unknown*

# Contents

# Appreciation

I would not be where I am today or have the freedom to do the things I am doing without the support of other people. There are many people who have brought much joy, challenge, focus, and opportunity to my life. I will mention only a few. My sincere appreciation is extended to my parents, Emanuel and Agnes, who, though they are gone, still live within me; my fabulous children, Skye, Jewelia, and Anouk; my wife, Bellsa, who brings great passion to her pursuits; my family members who have supported me in many positive ways at different points in their lives—Sandy, Karen, and Ron; and many excellent graduate students who over the course of my career have contributed in very positive ways and continue to play a meaningful role in my personal and professional growth.

Thanks to Laura McEwen for her excellent ongoing contribution to the Positive Living Skills Program over a period of many years, Brittany Glynn for her insights on focusing and positive living, and James Galipeau, Maria Jose Ramirez, Kathy Kearney, Lucy Mortimer, and John Coleman for meaningful interaction that enhanced the quality and relevance of this book; and Remi Simard for being there when I needed him.

Thanks to the many inspiring children, teachers, coaches, athletes, and high-level performers in many different fields who welcomed me into their worlds and inner lives. I have been honored to work and grow from your challenges, insights, and wisdom over the course of my life. I have learned something of real value from every child, parent, client, student, teacher, coach, and athlete with whom I have worked. They have kept me rooted in reality and are continuous reminders to make things positive and relevant for the real world.

And to the team at General Store Publishing House (*www.gsph.com*) for publishing, promoting, and distributing this book, *Positive Living Skills: Joy and Focus for Everyone*: Tim Gordon, Publisher; Alison Roesler, publicist; Jane Karchmar for her excellent assistance in the final editing process; and Magdalene Carson for her creative design contribution.

I am very thankful for the abundance of genuine, loving people with whom I have had the pleasure to interact at home and in many remote corners of the world. You have been my greatest teachers and have continually challenged me to find a better way. I thank you all for the many gifts you have bestowed upon me.

# Moving Forward

The Positive Living Skills activities in this book were developed from a deep commitment to meet the real and urgent needs of children, youth, adults, parents, teachers, performers, and billions of people around the world who are living through very challenging times. The Positive Living Skills educational program was developed through extensive field research with thousands of children, youth, and adults over a period of more than thirty years—with the help of primary school children; tweens and teenagers in middle and secondary schools; college and university students; children and adults facing life-threatening illnesses; children and youth with attention deficit disorders; high-level performers in sport and many other high-performance pursuits; leaders in business, government, and education; and adults from all walks of life who simply wanted to add quality, meaning, and joy to their lives and the lives of others.

There are many people, young and old, who have inspired my quest for more positive and practical ways to improve the quality of all human life on our planet. All with whom I have worked, played, or lived, and whom I have listened to or observed have become my teachers in some way. Those who were on a positive path inspired me to think of better ways to free more people to walk along on this noble path. Those who were on a less positive path challenged me to find better ways to free more children, youth, and adults to live with more balance, harmony, and joy in their lives.

Authentic positive change in our own lives and our larger world is a realistic goal. It begins with a positive vision of ourselves, valuing others, and seeing the possibilities of a better world. It is nurtured with an effective plan to help ourselves and others become more pure and positive, and a commitment to act in creative ways to turn our visions into realities. Collectively we have the capacity and the tools right now to make a positive difference in our own lives and in the lives of children and youth throughout the world. You and I, and millions of others who believe in a better world, have a unique opportunity, in our hands and hearts right now, to provide children and youth with meaningful positive learning experiences that will change their world and our world in meaningful ways, now and for the future.

As you read and feel the simple messages in the following pages, take a moment to reflect on the real possibility of turning existence into positive living for all people. Try some of the positive living skill activities yourself and with your loved ones. Think about how YOU can act and live in more uplifting ways. This sort of action is the most critical part of positive real world change. Thinking is not enough. Talking is not enough. Even Deciding is not enough. ONLY POSITIVE ACTION COUNTS. The action part of deciding, which I call "DOciding," is when you actually DO something positive to make the positive changes you are seeking for yourself and others. DOCIDE to become a key player in enhancing the quality of your own life, the lives of others, and the destiny of our world. Your personal life and our larger world depend upon it. We cannot accomplish this mission alone, but we can do it together.

If you are a teacher, parent, coach, leader, or workshop facilitator, use the activities and techniques provided to help your children, students, performers, or teams to DO something positive to make the positive changes they are seeking for themselves. Start a landslide of positive action!

Continue to embrace the simple joys and the simple opportunities and live the lessons from your journey.

## SIMPLE STEPS TO SIMPLE JOYS

Love is the heartbeat of life.
Appreciation is pure food for the soul.
Simple joys are the rays of sunshine
that light up each step of our journey.
The path to joyful living
lies in embracing simple joys,
simple joys that are all around you
and within you.
Look closely and you will find them.
Stretch out your arms and you will touch them.
Open your heart to embrace them.
Now is the time,
this is the place,
for living simple joys.
Seize each moment to love
life's simplest joys.
Dance with life.
Keep your heart open to life's magic moments.
Appreciate the good things in your life.
Share your appreciation with others.
Open yourself to opportunities,
and opportunities will open to you.
Embrace the special moments.
Relish the special memories.
Feel the Joy of anticipation.
Do what you would really love to do.
Move forward in life—proudly, freely, joyfully,
with your eyes and heart open
and your arms outstretched to the sky.

# 1

# POSITIVE LIVING SKILLS

*On what we do with children rests
the destiny of our world.*

## Three Gifts

If you could give three gifts to your children or the people
you love most in your life—gifts they can carry with them
for the rest of their lives—what would those gifts be?

My first gift would be **Positive Focus:** Skills that
empower children and adults to see the light in themselves
and in others, believe in their own capacity and that of
others, love good people and uplifting things in their life,
express their appreciation to others, and embrace simple
positive experiences every day.

My second gift would be **Connected Focus:** Skills that
free children and adults to "be" completely in the moment,
connect fully with each other and each experience, become

inseparable from what they are engaged in, and experience purity, joy, and meaning in everyday actions, interactions, learning opportunities, and performances.

My third gift would be **Less Stress** and **More Harmony:** Skills that free children and adults to embrace moments of silence, relax, release themselves from unnecessary stress or worry, and move forward through life with a spirit of inner harmony, pure joy, self-acceptance, and balance throughout their lives.

I choose these three gifts because they are clear and pure ways to nourish the heart and soul of humanity. Each of these gifts is dependent upon learning essential Positive Living Skills that nurture positive learning, living, and performance. These gifts empower us to enhance the quality of all human life—for children, teenagers, and adults.

The gift of positive and connected focus weaves its magic in all contexts, pursuits, and interactions—in quiet times, challenging times, and times of uncertainty. It opens the door to enhanced learning, improved performance, more joy, and greater harmony in life. The gift of less stress and more harmony impacts directly on the overall quality of all relationships, interactions, families, teams, and—ultimately—global harmony.

My three chosen gifts are essential to everything meaningful, good, or positive that we experience, pursue, or accomplish in life, as children, youth, and adults. They impact directly on the quality of every learning opportunity, relationship, interaction, family, team, and performance context that we enter throughout our lives.

If we simply bestow these "gifts" on our children, family members, teachers, students, partners, teammates, colleagues, coaches, educational and political leaders, and friends and enemies, the world will immediately become a better place to live, learn, love, work, grow, embrace, and enjoy—for everyone. Ultimately, harmony within ourselves, our families, our relationships, our homes, schools, and communities, as well as harmony with nature and global harmony depends upon learning and applying Positive Living Skills.

## Creating a Better World

I have a dream that many other people may silently share—I dream of a better world, a world of personal growth, harmony, and joy for everyone, a world where every person is free to live his or her positive dreams, where all people of all ages contribute to making their own lives, their own relationships, and the world a better place for all. I envision a world where we all embrace joy and harmony within ourselves, our relationships, our homes, schools, communities, and places of work—a world to which we all strive to contribute in meaningful ways. In this better world, mutual respect, love, empathy, and positive interactions replace negativity, disconnection, despair, neglect, abuse, and violence. Children and adults are nurtured to live and learn in more meaningful, joyful, and positive ways. People of all ages care about each other and help each other live closer to their true human potential.

In this dream of mine, people are more grounded, positive, loving, giving, and connected with each other, with nature, and with their experiences in positive ways. People are more appreciative of their own gifts, the gifts of nature, and the good qualities in others. Relationships are more positive, more fully connected, and more open to mutual growth. People live life from the core rather than skipping through life on the surface.

I know in my heart and soul that we are capable of creating this better world. I also know that this better world will only become a reality if people like you and me (in all parts of our world) open ourselves to this opportunity and teach children essential skills that are required to embrace a higher quality of life.

Living with more quality, joy, and harmony is a realistic possibility for every human being. Every day, you and I and millions of others can choose to do something meaningful to lift ourselves and others. A world of more vibrant, caring, creative people is certainly within our human potential, especially if we begin with ourselves and our children.

Positive real-world change at the individual and global level can begin right now by teaching children essential skills that empower them to live their lives in more positive and connected ways. A better world begins when you and I begin to teach children to value and respect themselves and their own potential, to value others at all stages and ages, to value nature and what it has to offer, to seek positive opportunities, and embrace simple joys every day. A better world begins by teaching children to focus on the positives—to focus on the good things within themselves; the qualities that live within others; and the reasons why they can, and how they will, achieve worthy individual and collective goals.

Becoming fully human is the most basic and essential human right for all people on our planet. All human beings are capable of contributing, of achieving worthy personal goals, and living their dreams. All people are capable of embracing challenges, focusing on the good things in their lives, turning negatives into positives, focusing on the step in front of them, and finding a way to make a difference in their own lives and the lives of others.

You and I can begin to create a better world right now by living in more positive and connected ways and by teaching children Positive Living Skills—one child, one parent, one family, one teacher, one classroom, one friend, one school, one community, one state, one province, one region, one country at a time. When millions of children and youth are supported by millions of other children and youth, as well as parents, teachers, leaders, and friends, global change becomes a reality.

# 2

# THERE'S TROUBLE
# IN PARADISE

*Every human being has the capacity to engage in human acts of kindness—every day. Why do so many people fail to do this?*

**E** very day, billions of people around the world waste huge amounts of positive energy because they focus on negatives or fail to focus on the positives—within themselves, others, and the world around them.

Every day, billions of barrels of opportunities, talent, and passion are wasted because people, young and old, do not focus in meaningful and fully connected ways. This directly affects the quality of all living, learning, performing, working, personal interactions, and relationships.

Every day, hundreds of billions of opportunities for embracing life's simple joys are lost because people have not learned to embrace the uncomplicated magical moments that are within their reach every day.

There are people who live in some of the most beautiful places on the most amazing planet in the universe who still feel unfulfilled, uninspired, unproductive, or unhappy. How can this happen? This happens when children, youth, or adults do not learn to see the positive qualities within themselves and others; or the opportunities for embracing simple joys in everyday experiences. This happens when people do not learn to connect fully with the good things in themselves, nature, and their daily lives.

Most people who fail to live close to their human potential have not learned to embrace the unique opportunities and possibilities that exist within them and their environment. We can all learn to live in more positive and meaningful ways—every day—if we simply learn to value ourselves, value others, embrace kindness, appreciate simple joys, and choose to live our lives closer to our true human potential.

Given the state of stress, disconnection, dishonesty, negativity, abuse, disharmony, and brutality in our world, collectively we are not doing a great job on behalf of our children, ourselves, or our world.

We really need to begin to collectively provide:

- Good role models for living in more positive, caring, and fully connected ways

- Effective educational programs for teaching children and youth to live in more positive, caring, and fully connected ways

Very few schools or educational institutions in the entire world are effectively teaching children or teenagers basic Positive Living Skills. If we want to live in a more positive world, it is absolutely essential to teach children and youth how to live and interact positively, learn effectively, perform to capacity, live in harmony, and embrace their true human potential. NOW is the time to begin teaching all children, all youth, all people, essential skills for Positive Living.

# A Troubled World

There are hundreds of millions of destructive acts committed by selfish, insecure, and misguided people in our world every day. We witness problems related to negativity, abuse, disharmony, despair, stress, brutal violence, wasted opportunities, and wasted lives on a daily basis. The major news networks highlight some of the most inhuman acts of our species every night and rarely highlight anything uplifting or positive. How do people arrive at the point of killing, maiming, abusing, and destroying innocent children and unprotected women in so many parts of the world?

Each of these people began his or her life as an infant with the capacity to engage in humane acts of kindness every day. How do young children grow to the point of hurting, shooting, stabbing, or massacring fellow students or innocent victims in schools, communities, training centers, even as members of what are considered civilized societies?

Some actions are so destructive that they inflict instant, life-altering consequences on innocent people, their families, and entire communities. Other actions, like negative comments, threats, put-downs, exclusion, or psychological bullying may not have immediate devastating effects, but when this continues on an ongoing basis, it can pick away at the victims' joy and self-esteem—every day. Small and large acts of negativity, especially when they are repeated over and over again, can lower self-confidence, motivation, productivity, belief in humanity, and the joy of living.

Even one person who is negative, uncaring, destructive, or unappreciative in a group or one-on-one situation can create an atmosphere of increased negativity, stress, or disharmony that is felt by everyone. If we can prevent this one person (and millions of other such individuals) from becoming negative in the first place (when he or she is a small child, teenager, or young adult) or turn him or her around by helping to shift focus from negative to positive, from uncaring to caring, from abusive to appreciative, everyone gains.

We have a choice here to take action—to try to change

something that has gone wrong—or to do nothing. Do we just accept this growing negative stream of inhuman behavior with its proliferation of greater threats, less empathy, more emotional and physical harm inflicted on innocent children, youth, and adults who are simply going about their daily lives? Do we just shrug our shoulders, do nothing, and begin to see this as the "normal" state of our communities and our world? Do we care that the age of those inflicting emotional and physical harm continues to get younger? Are we concerned that the age of those who are the *targets* of emotional and physical harm continues to get younger?

People who intentionally or deliberately cause stress, pain, or misery to others have failed to learn essential human skills for Positive Living. They are disadvantaged shells of what they have the potential to be, simply because they have not learned essential skills for being fully human. They do not see or nurture the untapped qualities in themselves. They do not appreciate good qualities in others. They do not interact with others in meaningful, caring, or respectful ways. As a result, they become obstacles to their own positive paths and also block the positive paths of others.

## Reason for Hope

One indisputable reason for hope is that young children do not begin life with negativity, hatred, or the goal of hurting, destroying, or blocking the positive paths of other human beings. Every child on our planet has the potential to become a loving, caring, contributing, appreciative human being. Every child can gain a definite advantage by learning Positive Living Skills at an early age. Acting locally on this simple, positive, global initiative will serve the best interests of every human being, in every corner of every country on our planet.

## Beginnings: Going Back Upstream

To solve the major problems we are facing in many schools, communities, and countries throughout the world, we need to go back upstream with a plan to prevent these kinds of problems from arising in the first place. If we teach young children Positive Living Skills and nurture them to become more fully human at the source, we will prevent or solve most problems before they ever become problems.

A young child is a pure and beautiful little stream of life. That child has the potential to become a loving human being. At its source, a small child flows gently, joyfully, innocently. He or she is like a tiny mountain stream of pure, crystal-clear water. In positive environments, little streams grow into powerful rivers, lakes, or oceans, and little children grow into strong, caring people who remain pure and clean. Children will continue to live, thrive, contribute, and grow toward their true potential when there is purity, positive connection, and meaning in their lives.

In negative environments, little streams and little people can become polluted, self-destructive, and destructive toward others. We cannot risk waiting for rivers or people to become polluted or toxic and then attempt to clean them up or enlighten their perspective. It is best to start when they are small, pure, clean, and free and open to grow in positive ways—and continue to support these positive ways of being as they continue to grow.

We cannot sit quietly and do nothing as we witness such disturbing and destructive events within our own rivers, oceans, and communities of life. We have to go back upstream and prevent these kinds of problems from surfacing in the first place. It is best to solve them at the source, before they become problems, or when they are still small and manageable. We can begin at the beginning by teaching young children to be positive, caring, and productive human beings and thereby give them the advantage of having more years to live, love, and contribute in positive ways.

## Flowing Forward

To begin moving forward, we need to ACT in more positive ways so that all children, youth, and adults have the opportunity to become what they have the potential to be. We also need to inspire others to ACT in more positive ways. If we fail to do this now in our schools, homes, and communities, the problems we are currently experiencing will continue to grow—for us, our children, our grandchildren, and future generations that follow.

Every child, teenager, and adult on our planet is worthy of living a positive, compassionate, and meaningful life, regardless of his/her place of origin, residence, language, cultural background, or level of income. Every child, teenager, and adult is capable of embracing the gift of life and making a meaningful contribution to her or his family, community, society, and world.

We can begin this journey right now by imagining what our children, teenagers, and adults have the potential to be and move forward from there.

**Imagine** . . . what our world will look like when every child, teenager, and adult in the world learns to:

- Focus on the positives

- Respect and value others

- Become what he/she has the potential to become

**Imagine . . .** what our relationships, families, and communities will feel like when every child, teenager, and adult learns to:

- Be Positive with him/herself

- Be Positive with others

- Live with empathy and compassion

- Pursue meaningful dreams

**Imagine** . . . what our classrooms, schools, quality of learning, working, and performing will be like when every child, teenager, and adult learns to:

- Focus fully in every learning context

- Focus fully in every performance context

- Connect fully in every personal interaction
- Focus fully on the process of pursuing his/her dreams
- Embrace the positives in every day

**Imagine . . .** what our lives, relationships, and world will feel like when every child, teenager, and adult learns to live with:

- More joy
- Less stress
- Genuine compassion
- Harmony and balance

**Imagine . . .** the real possibility of a better life and better world for all children, all teenagers, and all adults in every part of the world.

Every human being has the capacity to focus on the positives, embrace the possibilities, live the opportunities, and connect in more positive ways every day.

Every human being has the capacity to appreciate simple joys and simple interactions—every day.

Every human being can continue to get better at bringing out the best in themselves and in others.

Every human being can gain something of value by connecting in more positive and meaningful ways—at all ages and stages, and within all venues of life.

We can all choose to live with more harmony, balance, and passion in our lives.

We can all choose to embrace the simple joys in every day and help others to embrace the simple gifts in their lives.

This is within our control.

## Positive Action

Make a promise to yourself and others, right now, to take some simple, positive action steps to create a better world for yourself, your children, your family, and community. Make a promise to yourself to take some steps forward and then act on those simple initiatives.

When my youngest daughter, Skye, was six years old, she reminded me of the importance of honoring a positive promise: "A promise you make to yourself is still a promise—so you have to keep it."

Let's work together to turn our positive visions into realities for ourselves, our children, and people throughout our world.

*Let's take one action step forward every day to turn our positive dreams into realities.*

# ③

# LOVE, JOY, AND APPRECIATION

*Love, joy, and appreciation for life, people, nature, positive experiences, and worthy contributions feed the heart and soul of all humanity.*

I would like to share an experience about love that is still fresh in my mind and heart. During our winter holiday season, my family, and many other families, bring a tree into our homes and decorate it with lights and simple, beautiful ornaments. We do this to celebrate this season, celebrate each other, and reflect on what our world could be. Last night when we were completely absorbed in decorating our tree, my eight-year-old daughter said, "I love life." She said it in a soft and yet powerful way. It was as if she was thinking it to herself and the words slipped out naturally.

Just to be sure that I heard what I thought I heard, I asked her, "What was that you said?"

She said it again—a little louder—"I love life."

I stopped what I was doing, looked directly into her eyes, and shared what I was feeling: "Wow, that's really great. What a beautiful gift—to just love life!"

When is the last time you thought or felt that you really love your life, or at least parts of it? How many people do you know who can honestly say that they really love life, or parts of their life, every day? The potential for loving life is not restricted to young children and puppies. To really love life, we have to open ourselves to see life more like a child and embrace good things each day. We have to remain open to simple opportunities that can lift us every day.

## Open Yourself to Opportunities

I often run along a small trail through the forest where I live. One beautiful, sunny, autumn day, the green leaves on the trees were changing to brilliant shades of bright red, orange, and yellow. As I was running along, I noticed that when the wind blew, some of the colorful leaves floated down from the branches. I continued to run with my hands wide open, palms up, and my arms stretched out to the side. Within a minute, a beautiful little red leaf spiraled down gently and landed right in the center of my hand.

That leaf was a great reminder for me to remain open to opportunities. I didn't try to grab that leaf or even reach out for it. I just opened myself and my hands to that opportunity and it came to me. There are many good things or opportunities that can enter your life simply because you remain open to possibilities. If I had not opened myself to that little red leaf, it never would have fallen into my hand. It wasn't the leaf itself that was so important, it was the lesson from that leaf. If you remain open to opportunities, they will open to you.

I shared my leaf story during a presentation to people from many different backgrounds and cultures at a world congress in North Africa. The day after my presentation, a bright and energetic young man from Dubai tracked me down and said, "I have to tell you my story." He began by saying that he loved the leaf story and then told me about something special that happened to him shortly after listening to my presentation. He and a group of new friends from different countries were walking down the street together on their way to dinner. He was walking along with his arms stretched out to the sky and reminded his friends about the importance of embracing all the beauty around them. He approached a big tree on that street, slowed down and stopped under that tree to admire and appreciate its beauty. At that same moment, a huge bird perched high in this tree released an immense load of bird excrement that splattered down and covered the entire top of his head!

What could be positive about that? It was fortunate that he was not looking up with his mouth open wide when the bird delivered its gift. In some countries, bird droppings on top of your head are a sign of good luck . . . better things on the horizon. In the end, this unique experience led to a huge amount of laughter and a shared memory that brought this multicultural group together in a very special way. It also brought this bright young man to me to share his story. I will always remember him and his unique experience and so will he. Another lesson that emerged from this story is that although opening yourself to opportunities usually leads to something positive, not every opportunity leads to the positive outcomes you might expect. However, you can still find a lesson, grow from the experience, and move on to the next opportunity.

The day after I returned from Africa, I was running on the trails near my home and saw a beautiful little red leaf lying on the ground. I picked it up. That little leaf got me thinking about millions of other leaves and opportunities that fall to the ground and stay there. How many opportunities in our lives fall to the ground every day, every week, every year—and remain there—simply because we do not slow down or stop long enough to connect or open ourselves to those opportunities? Why not stop and pick up that little leaf, embrace that gift in your day or in some part of your life? As long as you remain open to opportunities in your life, they will open to you.

## Loving Life, Finding Joy and Happiness

There are thousands of reasons to love life. Love, appreciation, and simple joys bring meaning and moments of joyfulness to every journey and every life. Love is the heartbeat of humanity. Appreciation nurtures the human soul. Simple joys shine light on the qualities of each day.

There are thousands of little things to love and appreciate in life when you **choose to:**

- Open yourself to embrace life's magic moments — in nature, people, daily interactions, play, physical activity, learning, music, performing, and everyday opportunities

- Pause long enough to see and appreciate the wonderful little gifts that are all around you

- Appreciate the good parts of yourself, of others, of your experiences

- Connect more fully and more joyfully with people, daily experiences, nature, physical activities, and learning opportunities.

- Make good choices based on what will add joy, quality, and personal meaning to your life and the lives of others

- Do some good things that really lift you and your spirits today and every day

- Learn something of value about yourself every day that will make the days, months, and years that follow more joyful

The way to discover more love, joy, and appreciation in your life is to move through your day in a more connected and less hurried manner, with your mind and heart open to embrace every possible simple joy. *Happiness comes from embracing magic moments every day.* Not all moments are joyful, but there are joyful moments in every day. You simply have to open yourself to embrace those moments. Every day, every experience, every moment in your life happens only once—then it is gone. The moment you are living right now you can only live right now. Then it is gone forever. There may be other moments, other experiences, other days—but this day, this moment you are living right now, only happens now. The page you are reading right now, you will never again read for the first time or in exactly the same way. So read with full focus. Read it to remember. Read it to enhance the quality of your own life and the quality of the lives of the people you love.

## Why is it that some people who appear to have everything are not happy?

This includes many talented or wealthy people, including celebrities, leaders, heads of companies, successful students, and athletes, as well as millions of "everyday people" who might be smiling on the outside but feeling empty or unhappy on the inside. The reason that most people are unhappy is that they fail to fully appreciate the good qualities within themselves and in others, the good parts of their lives, the positive opportunities they have or can create, and the simple gifts that live inside them and are all around them. Unhappiness often begins to grow by failing to see or appreciate the gift of life or the simple joys or magic moments in each day. It is hard to be happy when you don't pause long enough to appreciate who you are; the good things you have in your life; the good things you have done, are doing, and can do; and the good qualities in others. Happiness becomes elusive when you fail to see positive possibilities for embracing simple joys and simple opportunities in your life, your world, and the world around you.

The door to a better life is opened when you open yourself to appreciate good people, good things, and the positive opportunities you have in your life; and when you share your love, appreciation, and best qualities with those around you—loved ones, students, colleagues, or others who can benefit and become more joyful from the positive things you can offer.

### When two people are living through similar circumstances, why is it that one person can be happy and the other person unhappy?

This usually happens because these two people bring different viewpoints into their life experiences. Happy people have learned to focus on the positives, not the negatives; on solutions, not problems; on the opportunities, not the obstacles. Unhappy people have learned to focus on the negatives, the problems, the obstacles—and do not see the opportunities. *The path to happiness and unhappiness is blazed by the focus you carry into each day of your life.*

Most people fall into the unhappiness trap for two reasons. They fail to appreciate who they are or what they have, and/or they always want what they don't have. The unhappiness spiral is ongoing for many people because even when they get what they want, they don't appreciate it because they now want something else that they don't have. Happiness becomes elusive for those who continue to dwell on what they don't have or don't like. Happiness becomes possible when people embrace the many "gifts" they do have and begin to fully appreciate or pursue the many things they do like. *Want what you have within you!*

### Why is it that some people who appear to have nothing are happy?

I have had wonderful opportunities to live and learn from aboriginal people in a number of different remote parts of our world. I visited a small jungle village in Papua New Guinea, which was like stepping back 1,000 years in time. The people lived in thatched huts, with no electricity, no running water, no modern appliances or technology of any kind. Barefoot children ran about laughing, playing, climbing coconut trees, and swimming in a nearby river. I joined in their play, learned their games, swam with them, and appreciated every opportunity to be with them and learn about how they embraced their lives.

That experience and many other experiences in other remote cultures made me really reflect on what frees people to be happy. These village people certainly did not have any material wealth as we know it. A big part of what freed them to live happily is that they really appreciated what they did have and did not know (or think about) what they didn't have. They were gentle and cooperative people who lived in harmony in a beautiful natural jungle environment where lots of fruits and vegetables grew readily. They fully appreciated the many gifts that nature gave them every day. They appreciated their children, families, and extended families. They respected their elders and even appreciated meeting a strange-looking visitor like me. These gentle people embraced the simple things and simplest joys in every day. This is what brought them happiness and harmony.

## The roots of happiness

Happiness takes root and grows when you focus on the positives, embrace the simple things you love, and appreciate the gifts you already have in your life. Happiness often demands that you slow down or literally stop, at least momentarily, to embrace life's greatest and most enduring gifts. Nature teaches us this lesson well. If you want to really feel the magic in nature—or the magic within another person, or within yourself—you have to stop, be still, and fully connect with the beauty, joy, or magic of that moment, without any thought of moving on or having to do something else. There are so many simple joys within reach every single day of every person's lifetime. We simply have to close the door to unnecessary stress and obsessive work or worry and open ourselves and others to fully connect with these basic gifts of life.

You, and those with whom you live, work, or play, can choose to fully appreciate the gifts you have in your life right now. It is a CHOICE that is nurtured by understanding that these simple daily gifts, which are often ignored, are in fact wonderful gifts worthy of embracing. Choose to focus on the positives in yourself, others, nature, and daily opportunities and experiences. Focus on being appreciative and thankful for whatever you have and have had. Focus on sharing your appreciation with others. Once you open this door, you will find many gifts of life—almost everywhere you look.

Every day, every experience, every new step in life is an opportunity to live, learn, love, grow, enjoy, contribute, or get better or wiser in some small way. Every day is an opportunity to do something that lifts you and lifts the spirits of someone else. Every moment is an opportunity to appreciate your life and what you have in your life. Every day is an opportunity to take one small step closer to how you want to be, where you want to be, and what you want to be.

### *Choose to:*

- Love more openly

- Appreciate more fully

- Trust your intuition

- Listen to yourself

- Create moments of silence

- Keep an element of playfulness in your life

- Hear the wisdom of others

- Enjoy, relax, and re-energize your body, mind, and spirit

- Embrace the simple joys in every day

## Nurturing Appreciation

Given the positive power of appreciation, it is important to teach children, youth, and adults to fully appreciate what they have and to openly express their appreciation to others. We all feel more fully alive when we open ourselves to positive opportunities, appreciate the opportunities we have, create new opportunities, appreciate others, and feel appreciated by others.

Most people live their lives without really appreciating what they have and without fully expressing their appreciation to others. Family units can live their entire lives without ever telling other family members how much they love or appreciate them. Children and youth can live their lives without hearing significant people tell them how much they love and value them. How often do you tell your children, parents, siblings, students, teachers, teammates, colleagues, or friends that you really appreciate them for being there for you when you might need them—or for just being there? When is the last time a family member, colleague, friend, teacher, or teammate told you how much he/she appreciates you? Probably not often enough!

Most people fail to fully appreciate what they have—especially when they have so much to appreciate. Too few people express their appreciation to others—especially when they have so many reasons to be appreciative of others.

When a friend, family member, or admired person dies, survivors usually find the time in their busy schedules to gather together and share what they loved or appreciated about this person, or at least reflect on what they valued or will miss about this person. Personally, I would prefer that people tell me how much they appreciate me while I am still alive, so I can actually hear it and benefit from it. There is great value in appreciating what you have in your life while you are still living, and also great value in expressing your appreciation to others while they are still living.

## *Express your appreciation*

How often do you take the time to tell people who have influenced you in a positive way that you really appreciate what they do or did for you? There are many advantages in expressing your appreciation to others—now. We all gain something of value by feeling good about ourselves and feeling valued by others. Even when we feel we are making a meaningful contribution to the lives of others, it is always nice when someone takes a few moments out of her day to tell us that she appreciates what we did for her or her loved ones.

When you share your appreciation with others, they feel valued and want to continue to do the positive things they are doing. When they share their appreciation with you, you feel good and want to continue to do the good things you are doing.

For most of my adult life I have worked and played with children; taught university students and worked with teachers, coaches, athletes, and graduate students; served as a focus coach with high-level performers; and helped many people pursue their dreams. I know that most of those people appreciated what I tried to do to help them, but it is rare that someone actually comes up to me or e-mails me and says, simply and directly, "I really appreciate what you shared with me/did for me." I really value the rare occasions when this does occur.

I distinctly remember a special appreciation moment that happened to me many years ago when I was playing cooperative games with a group of kindergarten children. At the end of that class, a very excited five-year-old girl came running over to me, tugged on my pant leg, and blurted out, "Terry, Terry, I really like you, 'cause you are nice on my feelings." That made me feel great! Even thinking about it now still puts a smile on my face. It would be great if we could all express simple, open, honest appreciation more often in our relationships, classrooms, families, workplaces, and the world at large. A little more appreciation as we move along the sometimes bumpy path of life can go a long way. We all appreciate being appreciated and feeling appreciated for the good things we do.

## *Act on your feelings of love and appreciation.*

Tell those special people who enter your life—whom you like or love or who like or love you, appreciate, respect, or support you, or lift your day or life in some positive way, how much you appreciate them. Share your words and gestures of appreciation, so they really know how much you appreciate them. "I just want to tell you how much I appreciate our connected time together—when you are fully there and I am fully there and the connection is fully there. This feels really good for me and is a constant reminder of how special you are and how special this connection is."

Expressing love and appreciation can enhance the lives of all people at all stages of life, from small children to well-seasoned adults. We all become more fully human when we value others and feel appreciated by others in return.

If you want your life and the lives of others to become more joyful, more complete, more positive, and more fulfilling:

- Open yourself to appreciate the good qualities in yourself, the good qualities in others, and the positive possibilities in your life.

- Express your love and appreciation to others.

- Continue to connect with special experiences that lift you.

- Continue to connect with special people who bring out the best in you.

- Continue to support yourself and others on your journey to more positive and meaningful living.

## *Beware the non-appreciation trap.*

Sooner or later, most human beings fall into the non-appreciation trap. Let me describe this through a simple story of a beautiful painting. A woman sees a beautiful painting; she is captivated by it and feels she cannot live without it. She buys the painting or acquires it as a gift and carefully hangs it on the best wall she can find in her home. For many days, she walks into her home, looks directly at that painting, connects with its beauty, and feels a sense of joyfulness and appreciation — just being in its presence. However, over a period of time, the painting remains the same but something changes. Now when the woman walks into her home, she doesn't even see it. She has, as they say, "tuned it out." She no longer appreciates its beauty because she no longer takes the time to connect with it.

This not only happens with paintings, it happens with people who are not hanging on walls, but who are in the same house, classroom, school playground, or workplace; as well as with almost everything else in life.

When I was visiting a quiet little remote place in Southeast Asia, I was staying close to a beautiful, long, white, sandy beach, where I went for a run and a swim very early every morning. I cherished my connected time on this beach with the sand and the waves and the feeling of running freely with the breeze coming off the ocean. It was very relaxing and uplifting and was a major highlight for me every single day. For me, the magic connection with nature never ends.

I spoke with a local woman in this village who had lived in this area her whole life. She told me that she worked very long hours, seven days a week, felt tired and stressed most of the time, was not sleeping well, and got headaches at night.

I asked her if she ever went down to the beach where I had been running. "Do you ever go down to the beach just to relax or walk along the beach with your toes in the sand and the waves rolling up onto the shore?"

She said that she used to go to the beach when she was younger but had not gone to the beach for many, many years. When she said this, it really surprised me, because she lived about a three-minute walk from this amazing beach. When I thought about it more, I realized that this was simply another example of someone getting caught in the non-appreciation trap.

A little walk along this beach with the waves rolling in would have really helped this woman relax and lift her spirits, especially if she did it in the morning as the sun was rising or in the evening as the sun was setting. It was a perfect place for gaining positive energy and perspective and for feeling a sense of connection and tranquility. It was a great place for anyone to be active, relax, enjoy, and connect with the wind, waves, and beauty of nature. It would have been an ideal context to put some balance back into an imbalanced or busy life. I am hopeful that this woman chose to embrace this simple opportunity to put some balance back into her life. I do know that it was within her control.

Almost anyone living anywhere risks falling into the non-appreciation trap. Whenever we stop noticing, connecting, or opening ourselves to simple joys and positive possibilities in our lives, we risk falling into the non-appreciation trap. Whenever we stop connecting in positive ways with people, nature, and daily experiences, we have entered the non-appreciation zone. This usually leads to unhappy days, weeks, or months, and sometimes the result is a lifeless life—not a great place to be.

The good news is that there are abundant opportunities in the real world to find meaning, joy, and positive connection—with nature, in many activities, and with many people. Most people who feel that positive experiences are unattainable in their lives are simply not connecting with what is available to them. When you open yourself to see and connect with positive possibilities, you begin to understand that they do exist. When you learn to connect in pure and positive ways with your own experiences, your own best qualities, and the best qualities in others, you become a happier and more fulfilled person. This will free you and those you love or care about to become better, happier, more fulfilled people.

## *Avoid the non-appreciation trap.*

Someone you know walks into his or her own home, school, neighborhood, or workplace and fails to acknowledge or connect with anyone. This person is living in the non-appreciation zone—at least in that context. The good news is, that person does not have to remain in that zone. The way out is simple and clear. When you see a family member, friend, colleague, someone you love or care about, or a person who needs a little support, simply "be there" with her or him, fully connected, for at least a couple of minutes. It doesn't take a lot of time to do this. If you are physically there, you might as well be there mentally. This means being fully focused and fully connected with that person at least for that minute or two.

Make an honest effort to connect fully with people when you first walk in the door or first see them in the morning, afternoon, or evening. Everyone appreciates and benefits from a positive greeting, positive connection, or positive interaction. Make it your goal to connect with good people in a sincere way that dips beyond the surface—every day.

Let those people in your life who give you positive energy know that you value them and their positive efforts. If you appreciate a person in your life, or parts of what he/she does, share your appreciation through your greetings, your connection, and the uninterrupted, meaningful moments you share with him or her.

## The Gifts of Love and Connection

There are many living paintings in our lives (many in the form of people) that we can continue to love and appreciate over a lifetime. These gifts do not leave us. We leave them. It is our willingness to continue to open ourselves to these gifts and to sustain a sense of connection and appreciation for them that keeps them alive. If you can simply sustain a pure connection with the simple and profound gifts in your life, you can sustain joy, appreciation, love, and meaning throughout your life.

The gifts of love, positive connection, appreciation, and simple joys are attainable and sustainable when you continue to connect fully with good people, positive experiences, and positive possibilities. However, these same gifts will fade or vanish if you stop connecting in positive ways—with people or with the uplifting experiences in your life. You cannot sustain love, joy, and appreciation for anyone, any place, any thing, or any experience unless you connect, reconnect, or continue to connect, in positive ways with special people, places, opportunities, or experiences. You CAN sustain love, joy, and appreciation in your life!

- Open yourself to an opportunity.
- Embrace a special moment.
- Appreciate something on a deeper level.
- Find, create, or build a special connection.
- Express your genuine caring or appreciation to one person.
- Learn something of real value today.

- Embrace a moment of pure joy.
- Don't wait until later. When you wait, the special moment is lost.

## Choose to Appreciate

Appreciate that you are here, you are alive, and you have moments to live remaining in your life.

Appreciate:

- Your own qualities, your personal victories, what you have accomplished through challenging times
- Good qualities in family members, friends, or supportive people around you
- Good qualities in classmates, teammates, colleagues, teachers, and people who care
- Meaningful relationships or parts of relationships (past and present), conversations, or parts or conversations
- People who have helped you in your life or performance pursuits and who are helping you right now
- The beautiful places you have visited, lived in, trained in, or performed in
- The simple, positive opportunities you have every day — to direct your life, make good choices, embrace the simple gifts of nature, and create new opportunities

This will free you to embrace the simplest gifts in life, and the gift of a more joyful life will come your way.

## Choose to Express Your Appreciation

Express your appreciation to people of all ages who make you feel good, do good things for you, lift your spirits, or enhance your day or life in some small or big way. Help other people feel more appreciated by expressing your appreciation in an open and sincere way. Everyone appreciates appreciation.

# Support Yourself and Others

## *Support yourself*

There is no advantage in putting yourself down, and lots of advantages in supporting yourself. So be positive with yourself, remind yourself of your good qualities, look for the things you do well, and know that you will be even better in the future. Look for the good parts of you, the good parts of what you do, and support yourself through the ups and downs of the journey. This will give you the best chance of feeling good, growing confident, improving from each experience, enjoying your pursuits, being successful, and becoming the person you really want to be.

## *Support others*

There is no advantage in putting down people, family members, friends, classmates, teammates, or colleagues, and many advantages in supporting them. So be positive with others, look for their good points, and support them in the good things they do. This gives everyone a better chance of feeling good, improving as a human being, becoming more respectful, communicating in more positive ways, enjoying other people, being successful, and becoming the person he/she really wants to be.

*Appreciate* who you are and the good people who support and appreciate you. Be grateful for the positive opportunities you have in your life, the good things you have done, are doing, and will continue to do in the future. Continue to take small, positive steps forward to become the person you want to become.

*Share your appreciation* with people who believe in you, support you, appreciate you, and continue to support the positive things you do.

## Embrace an Opportunity Today

- Find something positive.

- Embrace a simple joy.

- Become better or wiser in some small way.

- Become physically active in ways that reduce stress and free you to connect in joyful ways.

- Find moments of silence. Relax, rest, recover, and re-energize.

- Listen to your heart. Trust your intuition.

- Take one small step closer to living the life you want to live.

## Embrace Your Gift of Life

The fact that YOU are alive right now is a miracle and a gift. The day that you were conceived, 100 million sperm cells raced to implant themselves in a fertile egg. One unique sperm implanted itself in one unique egg—which created YOU. That victory gave YOU the gift of life. Millions of other sperm cells that started that race never lived to see the light of day. You won the gift of life that special day and for that you can be thankful every day. You owe it to yourself and others to make the most of your special gifts.

## Choose to Live This Day

Today you have the gift of twenty-four hours, 1,440 minutes, 86,000 seconds to live. It is within your power to live and enjoy some of these moments every day. Choose today to live sixty of those 1,440 minutes doing something positive that you really love or like to do—something that you find relaxing, something physical that you enjoy doing, something joyful or playful, something that brings you moments of silence and that frees you from other demands.

Choose today to live 300 seconds (five minutes) of those 86,000 seconds really connecting with a person you see, meet, care about, or interact with—where you are fully connected with this person and not thinking about anything else.

You only live this day once. You only live this moment once. You only live this life once. Don't waste the moment. Don't waste the experience. Don't waste the opportunity.

## Choose to embrace this MOMENT.

## Choose to embrace this OPPORTUNITY.

## Choose to embrace this GIFT OF LIFE.

### *Live this day!*

### *Choose to do one thing that you would love to do TODAY!*

## Do it!

# POSITIVE FOCUSING SKILLS

### *You are or become what you focus on.*

**F**ocusing is the most important skill in life because it affects everything you do, experience, and accomplish in your life. It also affects everything our children do, experience, and accomplish in their lives—all learning, all performance, all relationships, and all interactions; all joy, stress, and relaxation; all meaningful progress and all positive contributions in life.

Unfortunately, many of us have not had the opportunity to learn to focus in positive and fully connected ways. This can lead to major deficiencies, difficulties, and disadvantages in positive learning, performance, interactions, and contributions in life. People who do not learn to focus in positive and fully connected ways often become distracted, disconnected, or consumed by negativity, stress, anger, or self-doubt. A negative or disconnected focus clearly interferes with joyful living.

The simple fact is that learning to focus in more positive and connected ways enhances the living of life itself—for everyone. It is imperative that we begin to teach people of all ages, in all cultures, to focus in more positive ways now. This will enhance the quality of their own lives, the lives of others, and the overall quality of our world.

We will live closer to our true human potential and achieve our personal and global goals when we:

- Learn to focus in more positive and connected ways

- Teach others to focus in more positive and connected ways

- Embrace the opportunities we have and do not yet have

- Open ourselves and others to embrace new possibilities

- Learn from every experience

- Act on our lessons learned

- Create new opportunities for ourselves and others

We will free children and youth in our own families, schools, neighborhoods, and communities throughout the world to live, learn, and perform closer to their true human potential by teaching them positive focusing skills. These are the skills that are required to attain and sustain a positive and connected focus—and a positive and fully connected focus makes great things possible for all people.

## My Personal Journey with Focus

My life has been a journey of discovery that has revolved around focus—my own best and less-than-best focus, and the best and less-than-best focus of others. My life as a teacher, coach, researcher, writer, and consultant for performance excellence and life enhancement has centered on two main goals: helping children, youth, and adults to fully understand the power of focus in their lives; and helping people of all ages to effectively improve the quality and consistency of their own best focus so that they can perform their best and live a life of quality and joy.

My personal journey with focus began at an early age. My father came from a tradition of gymnasts and circus performers. As a child, circus equipment was a normal part of our yard—wires for walking across, trampolines, trapezes, high bars, rings, springboards, and hand-balancing equipment. I spent much of my early life learning gymnastics and performing with my family. I enjoyed the challenge and the way it brought our family together as a cohesive unit. At the age of six, I began performing as part our family acrobatic act—which included my father, mother, two sisters, and brother. I was the youngest and lightest member of the family, which usually meant I was at the top of the human balancing pyramids we built. In some of our family balancing stunts, my father would literally support our whole family on top of his shoulders.

I can clearly remember times as a child, slowly climbing over my family members to get to the top of our standing human pyramids. This was an exercise in focus. I vividly remember a time when I felt my father's body start to sway forward and backwards—when I was not fully focused on what I was doing. In that context, I learned quickly that my focus or lack of focus could literally bring the whole family down to the ground in a heartbeat.

I learned that it was essential for me to move slowly and deliberately in a very focused and balanced way. I needed to maintain my center of gravity very close to each family member as I climbed over him or her to successfully and safely reach the top. At that tender age I learned and felt in my gut the importance—and in some cases the urgency—of maintaining a positive and connected focus. I practiced keeping my focus centered on the right things until I was very good at it. I knew this was critical not only for me to perform successfully but also for my whole family to perform well and without injury.

When we traveled on the road with our family act, I learned other important lessons about being positive and adaptable that remained with me. For our road trips, my father built a trailer that we hitched onto the back of an old station wagon. The trailer looked exactly like a covered wagon from the old Wild West movies, except a bit longer. It was covered with rough canvas that was painted white. On the side of our covered wagon, my father painted in big blue letters, "The Famous Orlick Family." Talk about being positive!

We carried all our performance equipment in that trailer when we were on the road and emptied it when we arrived at the performance site. Then we slid two big sheets of hard plywood into the covered wagon, one above the other, and we slept in the wagon—all six of us! Three of us slept on the plywood on the lower level and three of us slept on the upper level. We were obviously living the life of luxury on the road! None of us ever complained about sleeping in that covered wagon. We all got along very well and really enjoyed our time together on the road. From those humble beginnings arose the spark for lots of additional lessons learned about the importance of positive and connected focus—not only for performing to capacity but also for maintaining a sense of joy, harmony, and balance in our lives.

## The Value of Positive Focus

The values inherent in a positive and connected focus are relevant to all people and all areas of life. A positive and connected focus brings people up. A negative or disconnected focus brings people down—in relationships, families, teams, communities, organizations, and nations.

One person with a positive, constructive, and connected focus (especially with the help of other positive people) can raise the spirits, hopes, confidence, performance, and lives of millions of people, families, teams, schools, organizations, communities, and countries throughout the world. One person with a very negative, destructive, or disconnected focus can do a lot of damage, not only to themselves but also to the lives and spirits of many others.

Teaching people to focus in positive and connected ways early and often has value in all areas of life because it directly affects all relationships, all levels and forms of education, all learning and performance, and all human interaction in all work contexts and sport, teaching, parenting, and leadership, as well as maintaining an element of balance and joy in life.

My adult life has centered on developing a deeper understanding of the value of positive focus and connected focus. This has taken me on a journey to discover more effective ways to teach and nurture essential positive living skills. I have worked with thousands of children and high-level performers, all of whom have helped me to better understand the process of learning positive and effective focusing. My goal has always been to enhance personal excellence and team performance and to help all people of all ages to live in more positive and fully connected ways.

Perhaps the most important lesson I have learned over the course of my life thus far is that if you want to achieve high-level goals in any field, and if you want to enhance the quality of your life and the lives of others, it always comes back to focus. Your focus drives your life, drives your learning, and drives your performance—for better or for worse.

Billions of people in our world would love to be happier, experience more joyfulness in their lives, have better relationships, and perform closer to their true potential. If given a choice, most people would choose to live their lives with more quality, perform closer to their potential, and help their loved ones live joyful and meaningful lives. The reason this does not happen more often is that most people simply don't know how to do it. There are others who simply do not believe that a positive or joyful life is possible for them.

If YOU want to make positive changes in your life, you have to stop long enough to think about your own life, reflect on what you would like to improve or change, and come up with a positive plan for action. You then have to ACT on that plan and continue to refine your actions until you get to where you want to be.

Few people take the time to reflect seriously on what they really want in their lives and commit to an action plan that creates sustainable meaning, joy, and happiness. Not many people understand the extent to which their focus affects their quality of life, learning, and performance, as well as the quality of other peoples' lives.

The Positive Living Skills presented in the remaining chapters of this book can take you down the path you want to go. These skills can be learned and perfected like any other skill. When you choose to focus in more positive and connected ways, you will enhance the quality of your life. When you teach children, youth, and adults to focus in more positive and connected ways, you give them the tools to enhance the quality of their own lives. It is never too early or too late to plant and nourish the seeds for more positive living. Plant those seeds right now and nurture them within yourself, your family, friends, students, and colleagues. ACT on your good intentions.

## Choose Your Freedoms

Choose the Freedoms (from the following list) that are most important for you right now. Free yourself to embrace them. See where it takes you.

Free yourself:

- To connect
- To be fully in the moment
- To clear your mind of everything negative
- To let go of everything irrelevant
- To trust your intuition
- To spread your wings and fly
- From forcing "It" (or trying to force something to happen)
- To choose to rather than have to (do or be something)
- To believe in yourself, your intuition, your choices, your path

- To do the things you want to do

- To become your performance (for the duration of your performance)

- To become the person you want to be

- From coercion or pressure from friends, family, partners, potential partners, coaches, media, or others

- From constraints that get in the way of living, loving, learning, and performing in the way you want to live, love, learn, and perform

Choose to:

- Move beyond your comfort zone and remain there (for as long as it takes)

- Do what you want to do and trust it will take you where you want to go

- Trust your feelings and discover where they take you

- Make choices that YOU want to make and ACT on them

- Know that everything you want lives within YOU and your choices

- Become what you are experiencing, doing, feeling, wanting, or longing for

- Make decisions based on potential gains rather than fear of potential losses

- Embrace energy gains (within yourself, from others, nature, and within your pursuits)

- Avoid energy drains (within yourself, by others, and within your pursuits)

Free yourself to act on your deepest intuition (about people, potential partners, activities, performance pursuits, and opportunities for personal growth).

Free yourself to embrace Simple Joys every day.

Free yourself to live your day and life without feeling manipulated, or being forced or coerced into doing things you do not really want to do.

Free yourself from doing things that do not add joy, quality, or meaning to your life (or the lives of others).

Free yourself to do things that add joy, quality, or meaning to your life (and/or the lives of others).

### *Free yourself to choose your own freedoms.*

### *Free yourself to choose your own path.*

### *Free yourself to be YOU*
### *—the you that YOU choose to BE.*

### *Free yourself to be whatever you have the*
### *capacity to be.*

### *Free others to be whatever they have the*
### *capacity to be.*

Freedom can be applied to every area of your life: freedom to learn, freedom to perform, freedom to love, freedom within relationships, freedom to live the life you want to live, freedom to be or become what you want to be or become, freedom to help others become what they want to become.

### *Free yourself to pursue your freedoms*
### *in a connected, committed*
### *—but not desperate—way.*

### *Freedom is free—not forced, not desperate.*

# 5

# POSITIVE LIVING SKILLS FOR TEENAGERS AND ADULTS

*What you do with your day, or parts of your day, is your choice. Make Positive Living your choice—every day.*

## How You Live Your Life Is Your Choice.

Choose to:

- Focus in more positive ways
- Focus in more connected ways
- Reduce the stress in your life
- Appreciate what you have in your life
- Embrace simple joys every day
- Contribute to others in positive ways
- Live a more balanced life

The Positive Living strategies and activities in this chapter were created to help you to enhance the quality your life and to help you to help students, family members, and others to improve the quality of their lives. Let's start with you first! Then we will move on to help others.

## More Positive Living

Positive Living starts with a simple decision to live the time you have and embrace the special moments in each day. I am challenging you to enhance the quality of your life over the next twelve weeks and to continue on this positive path for the rest of your life. This chapter provides the basic tools that will free you to do this.

Follow the positive steps provided and you will make more positive living a realistic possibility for you, your loved ones, and others. Begin this positive journey right now by reading this chapter and acting on the steps provided. It will take you places you may have never imagined you could go. You are worthy of this positive challenge. Your life is worthy of these positive actions, and everyone who is important to you will benefit from the positive steps you take.

This journey to more Positive Living has worked for thousands of other people, and it will work for you, if you simply give it a chance. Read this chapter with a focused intent to remember and act on what is most relevant to you. Respond to the Positive Living Reflections Questions and Positive Action Plans provided at the end of this chapter. Act on one positive initiative every day to enhance the overall quality and joyfulness of your life. Persist with drawing out positive lessons that will free you to live each day and each experience in more joyful and less stressful ways. *Docide* to do what will help you to live your life in more positive ways. Remember, "docide" means that you ACT on the positive things that you decide to do. You are worth it and your life is worth it.

## You Are the Driver of Your Own Life

You are the only person who can truly enhance the quality of your life. Other people can help you move along this path, but ultimately you are the one who drives and sustains the quality of your own life. If you open yourself to opportunities, new opportunities will open to you. If you choose to invite more quality into your life, you will open the door to living with more quality. If you choose to focus in more positive ways, your life will become more positive. If you choose to connect more fully with people and positive experiences in your life, you will become more joyful and more fully connected in all parts of your life. If you continue to embrace positive possibilities, positive possibilities will continue to enter your life.

You are the driver of your life. You CAN direct the course of your life in positive and meaningful ways. It's your life and you are capable of making it what it can be.

- Embrace your greatest gifts—your life and the lives of others.

- Value yourself and your accomplishments.

- Appreciate the good things and good people in your life.

- Find moments of silence to relax and reflect upon your path.

- Move through obstacles like a flowing stream.

- Continue to create positive opportunities.

- Live your life the way YOU want to live it.

## Energy Gains and Energy Drains

Positive Living is an ongoing balancing act between energy gains and energy drains. Energy gains come from love, kindness, appreciation, being positive, expressing appreciation, and embracing simple joys.

***Energy gains*** come from positive people, positive experiences, positive pursuits, and focusing in ways that make you feel good, happy, connected, relaxed, uplifted, valued, worthy, grounded, challenged in positive ways, and more fully alive. Energy gains come from living, working, studying, learning, training, or performing in positive environments, interacting with positive people, embracing positive possibilities that lift you physically and emotionally, and freeing yourself to relax in ways that re-energize you or give you positive energy.

***Energy drains*** come from an absence of love, kindness, and appreciation; being negative, stressed, fearful, or angry; and failing to appreciate or embrace simple joys. Energy drains come from negative people, experiences, and pursuits, and focusing on things, or in ways, that make you feel unhappy, disconnected, stressed, sad, devalued, unworthy, uncomfortable, unwelcome, incompetent, or less than fully human. Energy drains also come from living, working, studying, learning, training, interacting, or performing in negative environments or carrying a negative mindset into those situations.

Whenever you shift your focus to positive possibilities or enter positive environments, you position yourself to lift yourself mentally and physically, reduce your level of stress, and regain positive energy. Look closely at who or what *gives you* positive energy and who or what *drains* your positive energy. This will help you to move forward toward more positive living.

Think of a situation, relationship, activity, or pursuit that gives you positive energy. Why do you think this relationship or activity gives you positive energy? Try to engage yourself more often with positive people or activities or in positive contexts that give you energy.

Now think of a situation, relationship, activity, or pursuit you are engaged in (or have been engaged in) that drains your positive energy. Why do you think this situation drains your positive energy? Try to reduce your time with people, activities, or contexts that drain your positive energy, or develop a positive plan to not let those people or contexts affect you in a negative way.

The ideal energy enhancement situation is when your chosen pursuit, activity, or relationship leads to positive energy gains, and your activities or interactions outside that pursuit also lead to positive energy gains. If you are living, training, working, or performing in a context where there is a constant energy drain and no positive energy gains, it is probably time to make some kind of change. Your options are to change the situation if possible, change your view of the situation, or find another situation or context that provides you with more energy gains and less energy drains. Some experiences may not give you energy and they may not take energy away. This is okay at times, but we don't want to live too much of life in neutral.

Each of us has a limited amount of emotional energy that we can give away without receiving some positive energy in return. To prevent emotional energy drains, or recover from them more quickly, it is best to do something positive to replenish our positive energy—every day.

***Block off some personal time—just for you***—to rest, relax, recover, regenerate, reflect, and embrace simple joys that lift you.

***Create moments of silence every day*** where you can clear your mind from all other concerns and completely relax. Find some quiet spaces where you can be silent or reflect on your own path.

Moments of silence and pure relaxation, anytime, anywhere, are wonderful opportunities for positive reflection, positive regeneration, emotional and physical recovery, and regaining a sense of balance and perspective in your life. Nature provides many unique opportunities to add silence, joy, balance, and uplifting energy to your life. You can find strength, relaxation, and recovery in the beauty, tranquility, and power of nature. Look for beautiful places where you can embrace moments of pure connection, inspiration, and exhilaration. Look for tranquil spaces where you can embrace moments of pure connection and simple relaxation.

You can immediately increase your positive energy gains and reduce negative energy drains by living in the presence of uplifting people, increasing your time in activities or contexts that give you positive energy, and doing simple things that free you to experience good energy every day. You can also try to find something meaningful in all people and all contexts or try to initiate changes in energy-draining contexts so they become more positive for you and others—if you have the energy. It's your life and you are worthy of doing whatever it takes to make your life the best that it can be.

## Positive Energy Drains That Lead to Positive Energy Gains

There are energy drains that lead to positive energy gains. For example, if I go for a long walk, run along a beautiful beach, run through trails in the woods, go kayaking, teach a class where I feel I have made a difference, do an inspiring presentation to a large group, spend a day working with a team, do one-on-one consulting, or focus on writing this book for many consecutive hours—I feel good, uplifted, energized, and happy for having had the opportunity to fully engage myself in these positive pursuits. Sometimes I also feel tired in certain ways—but the overall feeling radiating through my mind and body is positive.

I always feel more fully alive after immersing myself in physical activities that I enjoy doing, especially in an outdoor setting. These experiences leave me glowing and emotionally uplifted because they are joyful and positive for me. No matter how tired I feel physically after some of these activities, I feel fulfilled because the experience itself leaves me with a sense of joy, accomplishment, and overall well-being. Pursuits and healthy activities that leave you feeling positive and uplifted are a wise choice for ongoing joyful living.

The pursuit of personal excellence and the drive to contribute something of value to others over your lifetime require a great deal of positive energy directed toward worthy goals. To sustain optimal levels of positive energy over an extended period of time, it is essential to continue to find simple joys and moments of pure relaxation to replenish your energy. If you drain a gas tank or battery in a car, you have to fill it up again to continue moving forward. When you drain your physical or emotional energy tank, you also have to replenish the energy you have lost. To perform and feel best over long periods of time, replenish your energy tank with something positive, joyful, and relaxing every day.

## Zenergy Moments

*Zenergy* is a simple word I created to describe positive energy that comes from connecting completely with simple, positive experiences. *Zenergy moments* come to you when you connect fully with simple joys, magic moments, relaxed breathing, and little time-outs, and slo-o-ow things down to free your mind of all other concerns. Zenergy moments are a great way to replenish positive energy every day. Zenergy connections, even when they are brief, give you energy and free you to focus in more positive and connected ways. Zenergy connections also protect you from draining your emotional energy tank over the course of long or hard days.

Long-duration performers (for example, marathoners, triathletes, adventure racers) replenish themselves with fluids, water, food, energy bars, positive thoughts, and a positive and connected focus during their events. They don't wait until the end of the race or the end of the day to replenish their physical and emotional energy. Replenishing your positive energy over the course of your day is also important for emotional and physical energy replacement.

# Zenergy Reflections

Regardless of who you are, where you are, or what you are doing, at the end of your day there is great value in reflecting back on the best parts of your day. The simple act of reflecting back on highlights or special moments in your day gives you positive energy and makes you feel good about at least some of the things you did or experienced. When you reflect back on the good parts of your day, it also frees you to see or feel some of the progress or contributions you are making and helps you to be more appreciative of the positive path you are on.

# Long-Term Energy Gains

The most sustainable long-term energy gains come from continuing to do things that make you feel good about yourself, being happy about your contributions, grounded as a human being, relaxed on the inside, confident in who you are, and happy to be alive. To keep the door opened to long-term energy gains:

- Respect your own feelings.

- Choose to do more things that make you feel good or uplifted.

- Choose to do fewer things that make you feel negative or emotionally down.

- Choose to do more things that make your body feel healthy and alive so you can continue to live, interact, play, and perform at an optimal level.

- Rest, relax, recover, and regenerate in positive ways every day.

- Find joy, meaning, and lessons for ongoing positive living in your daily activities, interactions, and pursuits.

- Continue to embrace simple joys and simple joyful activities every day.

# Long-Term Health Gains

When healthy people become unhealthy or sick, it is often because they don't take care of their own basic needs—too much stress, too little physical activity, not enough relaxation, and too few simple joys. To reduce the risks of becoming unhappy, unhealthy, or unproductive:

- Balance energy drains with energy gains.

- Embrace Zenergy moments every day through pure connection with simple joys in play, work, performances, relationships, and life.

- Find effective ways to relax and re-energize every day.

- Don't waste emotional energy worrying about little things that don't really matter.

- Don't waste emotional energy trying to change people who are totally resistant to change. Plant some positive seeds and move on to other positive initiatives. Come back when they are more ready and you are more ready.

You can reduce a lot of stress in your own life simply by choosing to live with less stress in your life and letting go of unproductive worry. Practice different ways of avoiding or reducing unnecessary stress in every day. This will make your life more joyful, your interactions more pleasant, and your immune system stronger, which will keep you healthier and happier and will protect you from a variety of illnesses. If each day you simply embrace the simple joys and let go of unproductive stress, you will free yourself to become the positive and joyful person you have the potential to be.

# Reduce Unnecessary Energy Drains

- Make wise choices and act on them.

- Reduce the stress in your life.

- Avoid situations that drain your positive energy.

- Stop wasting emotional energy worrying about things that are completely beyond your control.

- Focus on doing positive things that are within your control.

- Relax, breathe, refocus—on what is within your control.

## Embrace Zenergy Gains

These four simple steps will help you to gain or regain positive energy every day:

- Simply relax. Do something relaxing today.

- Simply find a simple joy. Do something joyful today.

- Simply move your body. Do something active today.

- Simply connect. Connect fully with someone you interact with today.

## Wise Choices

Wise choices add joy and value to your life and ultimately to the lives of others. If the path you are on is not adding joy and value to your life, or not moving you in the positive direction you want to go, then change something in your life or chart a new path. A path is only a path. You are not required to stay on it for the rest of your life. Draw positive lessons from every path and every experience and live the lessons you learn.

Wise decisions often come from taking time to reflect on your path—especially with respect to personal energy gains and energy drains. Is this pursuit, activity, person, animal, application, relationship, or choice going to add quality, joy, and value to your life and the lives of people who are important to you—or do the opposite? In the long run, will this choice likely result in positive energy gains or negative energy drains for you? Will it reduce your stress and add joy and meaning to your life or add stress and reduce the joy in your life? Think more than twice before entering or remaining in a context that you feel, intuitively, is going to be a consistent, long-term energy drain for you and others who are important to you.

When making important choices, be completely honest with yourself (even if you are not yet able to be completely honest with others). Ask yourself:

- Do I really want to do this?

- Do I have the physical and emotional energy to do this [or continue with this]?

- Will this be an energy gain or energy drain for me?

- Can I make this a positive, energy-gaining experience for myself?

- In the long run, will this choice lead to positive energy gains or energy drains?

- If there are short-term energy drains, are they contributing something of long-term value to me and others?

If you really want to do something and have the emotional energy to do it, then do it.

If you don't really want to do something or don't have the emotional energy to do it, then don't do it.

If you are a person who cares about other people (which I think you are) and find it difficult to say "no" to a request, even when you do not have the time or emotional energy to do it, I have a little advice for you. Remember that saying "yes" to long-term joyful living sometimes means saying "no" to certain requests, especially if they are energy draining. Remember that a polite "No—thank you" is sometimes the best choice. "I am not able to do what you are asking me to do at this time, but I appreciate your asking." It is a wise choice to delay taking on additional energy drains when what you really need is an additional energy gain. Choose wisely.

# Seven Simple Action Steps to More Positive Living

You are ready to embark upon your special positive living journey. Your success will be enhanced if you answer the following questions in writing or type your responses in a Positive Living document on your computer. For people who cannot read or write, or prefer to speak: ask them the questions, listen closely to their responses, and type or write down their responses in their own *Positive Living Journal*.

## *Positive Living Journal*

Many people with whom I have worked to improve the quality of their lives and consistency of their performance have gained benefits from keeping a *Positive Living Journal*. Even people who had never before kept a Journal felt they gained from this reflective process. When you write down your personal goals and your best focus and lessons learned, it helps you to plan a clear path, act on your plan, make ongoing improvements, keep track of your progress, draw out positive lessons from your experiences (good or not so good), and continue to improve the quality and consistency of your performance and your life.

Best results usually come from making entries in your *Positive Living Journal* three to four times a week, especially in the beginning of this process. This includes writing down the Highlights of your day, what you tried to do to add joy and quality to your day, what you did to focus your best and refocus if you got off track, what you did to reduce the stress in your day, and lessons learned for ongoing improvement.

Positive Living Journals can also include inspiring pictures, art work and other visual images, quotations, songs, or other positive reminders of how you want to be as a person and performer—positive, focused, balanced, capable, connected, strong, confident, grounded, excited, happy, energized, and relaxed.

One of my clients pasted an inspiring picture of herself

on the cover of her *Positive Living Journal*. She was sitting on top of a beautiful mountain, totally absorbed in the purity of the boundless landscape in front of her, and loving it. This picture inspired feelings of joy, fulfillment, and pure connection that helped her bring similar feelings of pure, relaxed energy into other contexts.

What kind of image, picture, memory, or vision of the future might bring that kind of feeling or focus into your day and your life? What would you like to feel like in your life? What would you feel like sitting on top of the "mountain" you choose in your life and loving it?

## *Positive Living reflections*

The first step to more positive living is to reflect on the quality of your life and what brings quality and joyfulness to your life.

Write or type your responses to the following questions in your *Positive Living Journal*.

1. What does Positive Living or living a joyful life mean to you?

2. What contributes to Positive Living for you or brings joyfulness to your life?

3. What are the real loves of your life? What are the simple things that really lift you or make you feel most fully alive?

4. When different people are living through very similar circumstances, why do you think some of those people are happy and joyful while others are not?

5. Rate the overall quality of your life right now on a scale from 1 to 10 (1 means very low quality / very little joy in your life, 10 means absolutely great quality / lots of joy in your life, and 5 is somewhere in between).

6. Rate your overall quality of life in terms of what you have the *potential to be* on a scale from 1 to 10.

## *What you can do to enhance the quality of your life*

The second step to more positive living is to reflect on what you can do to enhance the quality of your life, why it is important, and what you have to focus on to do it.

Write or type your responses to the following questions in your *Positive Living Journal*.

1. What can you do, change, improve, focus on, or act on right now and over the next twelve weeks to enhance the quality or joyfulness of your life?

2. Why is doing this a worthy goal for you?

3. Why is doing this a worthy goal for the people you care about?

4. What are some good reasons for you to believe that you can enhance the quality and joyfulness of your life?

5. What do you have to focus on — or act on — to enhance the quality of your life?

6. How can you get yourself to take small positive steps forward toward your worthy goal(s) every day?

7. What are some positive reminders you can use to get yourself to act on your good intentions?

8. What are you going to do TODAY to take a step closer to your Positive Living goals?

## *Action plan for more positive living*

The third step to more positive living is to write down a specific action plan that you are going to start on today to enhance the quality of your life.

Write down or type your responses to the following questions in your *Positive Living Journal*.

1. What am I going to do today to enhance the quality or joyfulness of my day?

2. What am I going to do today to stay focused on the positives?

3.  What am I going to do today to create or embrace a positive opportunity?

4.  What am I going to do today to stay fully focused on something I am doing or fully connected with someone I am listening to or interacting with?

5.  What am I going to do to refocus if I start to lose my positive or fully connected focus?

## Bottom-line focus reminders for Positive Living

The fourth step to more positive living is to write down some simple focus reminders that will help you ACT in positive ways to enhance the quality of your life.

Write down or type your Focus Reminders in your *Positive Living Journal*. Read them over whenever you need a little reminder.

What are some Bottom-Line Focus Reminders that you feel will help you make this day, game, activity, class, learning opportunity, performance, or interaction as good as it can be? (Some examples might include: **Focus, Connect, Relax, Stay Focused, Refocus, Be All Here, Stay Positive, Find a Simple Joy.**) Choose your own Focus Reminders by drawing upon words, images, thoughts, or feelings that you feel will work best for you. Record these in your journal.

## Prepare yourself mentally to implement your positive living action plan so that you can live, interact, and perform in more positive ways.

The fifth step to more positive living is to get yourself mentally ready to act in specific positive ways BEFORE you start your day.

This is a very important step in helping you to live, learn, interact, and perform in more positive ways every day. Before you go to sleep at night or before you get out of bed in the morning, while you are still lying in bed, ask yourself the five questions in the *Action Plan for more positive living* (pages 52-53). This will serve as a great positive reminder for living closer to your full potential every day.

### Focus on why you can and how you will be successful with more positive living.

The sixth step to more positive living is to focus on why you can and will enhance the quality of your day and life.

Write down or type in your *Positive Living Journal* **why you can and how you will enhance the quality of your day**. These are your Reasons to Believe. Read them over whenever you need a little positive reminder.

The path to more positive living is cleared by making good choices, planning a positive path, and focusing on reasons to believe in yourself and your mission.

- **Focus on why you can enhance the quality of your life**. This will strengthen your belief in who you are, what you can do, and what you can become.

- **Focus on how you will enhance the quality of your day.** This will direct your focus in positive ways that will lead you to your goals.

- **Focus on connecting in positive ways.** Embrace simple, joyful moments every day. This will lift the quality of everyday activities.

### Don't just think about it—DO IT.

### Don't just say you will do it—ACT ON IT.

### Don't just do it once or twice —DO IT EVERY DAY.

### At the end of each day, remember your positive experiences and reflect on lessons learned.

The seventh step to more positive living is personal reflection on the worthwhile things you did each day and the lessons you learned from your best and less-than-best experiences that can be applied another day.

At the end of each day, think about your Highlights (Chapter 6). Think about the most fully connected moments in your day. Share your Highlights with friends, family members, teammates, and others. Ask them to share their Highlights with you. Look for positive lessons in the things that went well, and not so well, in your day. This will keep you on a positive path where you are living and learning more fully, appreciating more completely, and experiencing something meaningful, uplifting, or joyful every day.

## PERSONAL REFLECTIONS FOR ONGOING POSITIVE LIVING

1. What did I do (or try to do) today to enhance the quality or joyfulness of my day? Did I act on the positive things that I planned to do?

2. What did I do (or try to do) today to feel my best and stay focused on the positives? Did I focus on the positives?

3. What did I do (or try to do) today to stay fully connected with what I was doing? Was I fully focused on my listening, learning, performing, or other activities? Was I fully connected in my personal interactions?

4. If I began to lose my positive focus or fully connected focus, was I able to refocus quickly? If so, how did I do it? If not, what might help me refocus better or quicker next time?

5. What did I learn today that can help me be better, more positive, more focused, more connected, more relaxed, or more joyful tomorrow?

6. Did I use my positive focus reminders effectively to help me relax, focus, sustain my focus, or refocus today? If so, how did I do that? What worked? Can I get better at using my positive focus reminders, practicing my positive focus reminders, or finding more effective positive focus reminders? If so, how am I going to do this?

Ongoing positive living is made possible by persisting with your positive actions, continuing to draw out positive lessons for more positive living, and choosing to ACT on your lessons learned. This journey will lead you to meaningful positive changes in your life. Begin right now. Your life is worth it!

# Positive Living
# Is Grounded in Positive Action

The quality and direction of your life and the lives of those around you depends on making good choices and committing to positive actions. Good intentions are not enough to enhance the quality of your life. To live your life with quality, joy, and meaning and help others to do the same, only positive action counts—sustained, ongoing, positive action.

If you want something in your life to change, YOU have to change something. You can enhance the quality and direction of your life right now by focusing on your good qualities, the good qualities in others, unique opportunities, and embracing simple joys that can lift you in simple ways—every day. Decide to live in positive ways today.

Choose to:

- Live simple joys today and every day

- Focus on the positives

- Connect fully in your daily pursuits

- Value yourself and your accomplishments

- Appreciate and support others

- Focus on simple steps and simple successes

- Find positive lessons for more joyful living every day

- Pursue your dreams

If you guide your focus in positive ways every day, you will change your life in positive ways every day. What positive choices will you make today? What positive actions will you take tomorrow and the next day? Will you ACT on your positive intentions or just think about them? You Docide!

# Make Positive Living a Part of Your Everyday Life

A student in one of my university classes who wanted to make some changes in her life followed the Positive Living guidelines presented in this chapter. She sent me the following unsolicited e-mail a few months later.

> *I am writing to thank you for the joy your teachings have brought to my life. You have given me the tools to uncover happiness, pleasure, and relaxation that I never chose to focus on before. My relationships with my parents, siblings, and friends have changed significantly. To date I have continued my positive living journal and write highlights daily. I continue to challenge myself to live a more fulfilled life each and every day. There is so much I have learned. From the bottom of my heart I want to thank you.*

The steps to more positive living that are outlined in this chapter are very simple and very effective. If you simply commit to ongoing, positive, focused action and continue to act on positive lessons learned, you will change your life in worthwhile ways forever. You have everything to gain and nothing to lose by moving along this positive path. I wish you, your loved ones, and those who learn from you the best in this most noble quest.

# Focus Reminders for Positive Living

*Focus in positive and connected ways*. This will directly affect the quality of everything you do or experience in your life—your choices, learning, performance, interactions, relationships, joyfulness, relaxation, balance, achievements, contributions, and ongoing learning in life.

*Refocus in positive and connected ways*. This will directly affect how long you remain negative, distracted, angry, unhappy, disconnected, or emotionally drained before regaining a positive and connected focus.

*Persist with focusing and refocusing in positive and connected ways*. This will allow you to act on your good intentions consistently. You are or become what you focus on—as a person, learner, performer, family member, teammate, partner, leader, community member, and citizen of the world.

If you focus on positives, you become more positive.

If you focus on negatives, you become more negative.

If you focus on connecting fully, you become more fully connected.

If you focus on distractions, you become more distracted.

If you focus on relaxing, you become more relaxed.

If you focus on worrying, you become more worried.

If you focus on connecting fully, you become more fully connected.

If you focus on distractions, you become more distracted.

If you focus on what is within your control, you gain more personal control.

If you focus on what is beyond your control, you lose personal control.

If you focus on possibilities, you open the door to possibilities.

If you focus on impossibilities, you close the door to possibilities.

If you open yourself to new opportunities, opportunities will open for you.

If you close yourself to opportunities, opportunities will close for you.

If you focus on why YOU CAN—you probably will—because you are directing your focus in positive ways that free you to achieve your goals.

If you focus on why you can't, you probably won't—not because you can't but because you are focusing in negative ways that prevent you from achieving your noble goals.

## KEY REMINDERS
## FOR POSITIVE AND JOYFUL LIVING

**Only Positive Focus:** Only positive focus helps you to continue to learn, improve, and accomplish the great things you are capable of doing. So focus in ways that help you and others remain positive so you can embrace your life and accomplish your worthwhile goals.

**Only Connected Focus:** Only when you are fully connected with what you are doing can you live, learn, and perform to your potential. So stay fully connected with the little steps that free you to live joyfully, learn quickly, and perform your best.

**Only Positive Images:** Only positive images of doing the things you want to accomplish will help you to accomplish them. So imagine yourself doing the great things you want to do, exactly the way you would like to do them—with joy, connection, and confidence.

**Always "I Can":** There is no advantage in approaching learning, performance, or life situations thinking "I can't" or "maybe I'll mess up." So approach every learning, performance, and life opportunity thinking only "I CAN." ACT like you can, even if you are not really sure you can. This will give you your best chance of achieving your goals and living your dreams.

**Always "We Can":** When pursuing goals with teammates, friends, partners, family, and co-workers, there is no advantage in thinking "we can't." So commit yourselves to think, believe, and focus on "WE CAN." We can always be positive and connected in ways that help us to be our best. We can always learn and grow from every experience. "We Can" gives us our best opportunity to be successful and reach our personal and "team" goals.

**Always Opportunities:** There are opportunities in everything you see, do, or pursue to learn, grow, stretch limits, see openings, know yourself, understand others, overcome challenges; become stronger, wiser, more balanced, more accomplished, more consistent, more compassionate, more focused, and more human. So continue to look for positive opportunities and lessons in everything you see, touch, feel, and do.

**Always Lessons:** In learning, performing, and personal growth, there are no intentional errors, there are only lessons for improvement. So stay positive with yourself, no matter what happens. Be sure to look for the good things you have done, draw out the positive lessons and act on those lessons so you continue to grow, improve, and enhance the quality of your learning and performance, the quality of your life, and the lives of others.

**Make Positive Living YOUR CHOICE every day.**

# HIGHLIGHTS FOR POSITIVE LIVING

*Highlights are simple positive experiences, connections, actions, or interactions that bring joy, quality, and meaning to your life. Highlight connections free all human beings to live in more positive and joyful ways every day.*

Highlights are like going through your day with a magic marker and highlighting the best parts. (Seven-year-old)

Highlights are things that let your good feelings come out each day. (Seven-year-old)

A Highlight is something that makes you feel good, like giving your friend her birthday present. (Five-year-old)

Highlights are the opposite of lowlights. (Six-year-old)

Highlights are good things you can think of if you're feeling bad to make you realize it wasn't that bad a day. (Twelve-year-old)

## Why Are Highlights Important?

Highlights are important because they directly affect the quality and joyfulness of every day—for you, your children, and every other person on our planet. Highlights bring sustainable moments of joy to all human beings.

## Where Do Highlights Come From?

Highlights live within simple daily experiences and life's greatest challenges. Highlights come from embracing simple positive experiences, feelings, and pursuits that make you and others feel good, happy, uplifted, or better in some way.

## Why Teach Children, Youth, and Adults to Embrace Highlights?

Everyone who learns to embrace simple daily Highlights will add quality and joyfulness to his or her life. When children and youth begin to connect more fully with simple joys (Highlights), they begin to feel the immediate effects of a positive, fully connected focus. This positive focus can free all of us to live in more positive and joyful ways—every day.

## What Can YOU Do Today to Enhance the Quality of Your Own Life and the Lives of Others?

1.  Read the rest of this chapter and chapter 7 ("Highlight Activities"), with the intention of acting on what you are reading.

2.  Do some of the Highlight activities presented.

3.  Docide to look for and connect with more simple Highlights every day.

4.  Encourage others to find and appreciate more simple Highlights every day.

Each of us begins at a different departure point with respect to the number of Highlights we experience each day. When groups of children, teens, or adults are asked to share their Highlights from the past few days, some will share many different Highlights and others will say that they had no Highlights—nothing good, nothing uplifting, nothing joyful in the past few days.

Our research and experience with Highlight enhancement programs clearly show that regardless of where people start, they are capable of enhancing the quality and frequency of their Highlights within a short period of time. We often begin our Highlight sessions by talking about what Highlights are for different people and ask participants to share some of their favorite Highlights with each other. We often end our Highlight sessions by reminding everyone to try to find as many simple Highlights as they can (when they leave) so they can share their Highlights with us the next time we meet.

The simple process of getting people more engaged in looking for Highlights, writing them down, remembering them, and sharing them almost always results in an immediate increase in participant Highlight experiences (often within a day or two, or certainly within a week or two). Participants begin to actively look for Highlights. They open themselves to appreciating simple joys in their daily lives that they have often been ignoring, not connecting with, or not appreciating. Once people start down this positive path, the frequency and sources of Highlights continue to grow—especially with a little outside encouragement. In our school-based Highlight intervention programs, participants experienced significant increases in Highlights over a period of twelve weeks.

These positive gains become quite consistent if participants are encouraged to continue to look for and share Highlights.

Active participants in our Highlight enhancement programs begin to see their world, their daily opportunities, and their lives in a much more positive light. They reported feeling better about themselves as people, which was grounded in the fact that they were finding more positive things every day and were sharing Highlights with others. When children, youth, or adults begin to experience, write down, remember, and share Highlights that lift them, their view of themselves and their world begins to change in life-enhancing ways. It is much easier to feel positive, happy, and worthy (as opposed to feeling negative, unhappy, or worthless) when you focus on finding the positives in your day and your life.

## Sources of Highlights

Seven major sources of Highlights emerged from our extensive research with Positive Living Skills. They are self-generated and available in some form to virtually all human beings, almost every day. I place them on the "Wheel of Highlights":

- Positive Human Interaction
- Positive Interaction with Nature
- Positive Connection through Play, Games, Sport, Physical Activity
- Positive Personal Accomplishments
- Positive Personal Discovery or Creativity
- Positive Physical Sensations
- Pure Relaxation

### Positive human interaction

Pure connection with other human beings: a simple smile that lights up a special connection or good feeling within you or between you and another person; shared laughter; focused listening to another; a helping hand; a caring heart; a simple expression of love, respect, or appreciation; a genuine positive comment; sharing positive moments or special memories with friends, new acquaintances, or loved ones;

## WHEEL OF HIGHLIGHTS

connected time with people you like or love; feeling someone values you or cares about you; giving or receiving positive energy from someone; a warm hug or simple embrace; snuggling with someone who enjoys snuggling.

Open yourself to special connections with another person that go beyond the surface. Make time today to really "be" with a family member, friend, loved one, teammate, colleague, or acquaintance to relax, enjoy, connect, or reflect.

## Positive interaction with nature

Pure connection with the magnificence, power, tranquility, and positive energy of nature: a beautiful beach, expansive ocean, calm lake, flowing stream or river, mountain; a forest, tree, meadow, jungle, desert, garden, flower; blue sky, fluffy cloud, sunrise, sunset, moonlit or starlit night; sparkling crystals glistening like diamonds off the surface of a lake, ocean, or field of snow; the warmth of a campfire in an outdoor setting; quietly connecting with animals or birds soaring freely with their wings outstretched in the sky.

Open yourself to look closely for the simplest gifts and stunning artistry of nature. Open your sensory gates to connect with the abundance of simple joys and uplifting Highlights that can be found in nature every day.

## Positive connection through play, games, sport, physical activity

Pure connection through play, playfulness, movement, or physical activity that brings a heightened sense of joy, excitement, or personal well-being; play, laughter, and creative movement that brings children, families, friends, or teammates together in positive and joyful ways.

Open yourself to engage in physical activities and playful experiences that create opportunities for you and others to feel special, joyful, energized, happy, or uplifted in simple but meaningful ways. Seek pure connection in play or by engaging in physical activities.

## Positive personal accomplishments

Pure connection with the experience and feeling of achieving personal goals that are important to you (big or small); learning or accomplishing something that makes you feel good, valued, important, or worthy; setting a personal positive goal and attaining it; feeling good about moving one step closer to your goal; learning something new, meaningful, or exciting; feeling a sense of personal growth, personal improvement, or personal meaning; doing something (even one thing) well each day; finding an answer, solution, or direction you have been seeking; trying your best, doing your best, feeling your best, or being your best; feeling you are making a meaningful contribution to your own growth or the growth of others. Open yourself to appreciate the simple, good things you do every day. Rejoice in taking simple, positive connected steps that move you in the direction you want to go in the different aspects of your life.

## Positive personal discovery or creativity

Pure connection with the process of discovering, designing, creating, or constructing something new, exciting, special, or meaningful for you or others; discovering a new way or finding a new path; growing in positive ways through personal reflection on your dreams, actions, interactions, observations, feelings, contributions, or performances; dancing, singing, acting, making music, drawing, painting, making pottery, designing, writing, directing, doing photography, making films, or performing in a vast array of creative ways; engaging in personal discovery through reading, writing, listening, traveling, experiencing or creating something interesting, novel, exciting, fun, or meaningful to you and others.

Open yourself to pure connections with ongoing discovery, creative possibilities, and life-enhancing learning.

## *Positive physical sensations*

Pure connection with positive physical sensations that make you and your body feel good: the warmth of the sun on your face; a refreshing swim; the feel of cool or warm sand on your bare feet; a gentle breeze on your skin; a favorite meal, dessert, or cool glass of water on a hot summer day; wearing favorite clothing or slipping into bed with fresh, clean sheets; positive sensual connections with a person you like or love; the special feel of a gentle touch or mutually desirable loving embrace; a cleansing shower, relaxing massage, hot tub, or bubble bath with candles. Open yourself to the possibility of experiencing a variety of simple, uplifting, positive physical sensations that can lift your spirits and make you feel more fully alive.

## *Pure relaxation*

Joyful moments of pure, uninterrupted silence that make you feel completely calm, tranquil, rested, and peaceful in your mind and body; slowing everything down; taking a quiet repose or time-out just for you because you need it and deserve it; clearing your mind of all distracting thoughts to relax, be silent, connect, quietly reflect, or free yourself to enter a wonderful, restful sleep. Open yourself to experience simple moments of silence and embrace some form of pure, restful relaxation every day.

These seven major sources of Highlights included on the Wheel of Highlights are self-generated and available to virtually all human beings in all cultures, at all income and educational levels.

Entertainment was another source of Highlights identified by some participants in our studies. It was not included as one of the seven major sources of Highlights on the Wheel of Highlights for the following reasons: Participants were often spectators at events as opposed to being active participants; it was reported less often as a source of Highlights by children, teens, and adults in our studies; it was not as self-generated or readily available to all human beings on a global level. However, when it is uplifting and accessible, it is still a meaningful source of Highlights.

### *Positive entertainment*

Joyful feelings generated through listening to favorite music or songs; watching favorite movies, TV programs, plays, shows, or performances (dance, music, circus, sporting events, etc.); reading a great book; listening to a great story, speaker, or entertainer; shopping for something that makes you feel good or gives you positive energy. Open yourself to experience simple, positive Entertainment Highlights that have the potential to lift your spirits or give you positive energy.

## Pure Highlights

Pure Highlights are purely positive. They make you and others feel good, happy, accepted, connected, valued, and more fully alive. Pure Highlights are beneficial to you, your body, your spirit, your mental and physical health, your overall well-being, and the well-being of others. Pure Highlights have the special quality of lifting you and others without having a negative or destructive impact on you or anyone else. Actions, interactions, events, or products that are destructive to you or others (mentally, physically, emotionally, or spiritually) are not pure Highlights.

If everyone is encouraged to embrace pure and simple Highlights in everyday activities and interactions, we will increase the quality of all people's lives. Each of us can find and appreciate more simple joys in our days and lives. We can all learn to focus more fully on the positives and less frequently on the negatives. This simple shift in focus—from dwelling on the negatives to embracing the positives—will enhance the quality of billions of lives every single day. This is the simplest, most direct, and sustainable path to sustainable positive energy gains in our homes, relationships, activities, communities, and world.

# What about Lowlights?

Lowlights are the opposite of Highlights. Everyone experiences Lowlights on some days or at some junctures in their lives. Lowlights have the potential to drag people down and leave them feeling negative, distressed or unhappy. However, if you reflect in positive ways on Sources of Lowlights in your life, you can help yourself and others to reduce the frequency and duration of Lowlights and turn some Lowlights into positive lessons or Highlights.

## *Sources of Lowlights*

- Negative or absence of positive human interaction

- Negative or absence of positive interaction with nature

- Negative or absence of positive play, games, sport, or physical activity

- Negative or absence of experiencing positive personal accomplishments

- Negative or absence of experiencing positive personal discoveries or creativity

- Negative or absence of experiencing positive physical sensations

- Negative stress and/or absence of pure relaxation

- Negative or no positive entertainment

Lowlights come from negative experiences, actions, interactions, or inaction. They also come from focusing in ways that make you and others feel stressed, angry, unhappy, unappreciated, worthless, left out, hopeless, or emotionally drained. Sometimes we cannot control events that happen in our lives; for example, when someone else is negative, something goes wrong, we fail to achieve a goal, or lose someone who is important to us. However, we can control how we react to those events and we can learn from them.

Some people feel down, stressed, or negative because they are not connecting with the positive opportunities available in their lives. Often all they need to do is focus more fully on connecting with the possibilities that are already available in their lives. Some people feel down, stressed, or negative because someone, something, or some circumstance in their lives is negative. Sometimes this can be resolved by getting out of a negative or degrading situation, changing how they see or focus in a particular situation, helping another person become more positive, sharing time with more uplifting people, or engaging in more meaningful activities or contexts.

Finding more Highlights does not necessarily mean that Lowlights are eliminated from your life—unless you address, manage, reduce, or eliminate those Lowlights. However, Highlights can free you from Lowlights for certain periods of time and put some balance or perspective back into your life. Highlights can also help you see and manage Lowlights more calmly and effectively. Sometimes if you simply become more aware of your personal sources of Highlights and Lowlights, you can begin to embrace more Highlights and avoid more Lowlights in your everyday life.

## Everyone Can Find More Highlights

Our research with Highlights has clearly shown that when we teach children, teenagers, and adults to look for pure and simple Highlights every day, they find more positive things in each day and as a result they begin to feel better about themselves, more positive about others, and happier in living their lives. We are all capable of finding and appreciating simple joys—every day. We all have the capacity to respect ourselves and our personal needs. We all have the capacity to learn and show respect and compassion for others.

To move along this positive path, open yourself to the vast potential for Highlights within yourself, your experiences, other people, and different contexts. Look for High-lights within all the major sources of Highlights.

Open yourself to find Highlights during challenging or difficult times. This is a great way to begin to put things back in perspective. When I have experienced setbacks or loss, I have often gone to peaceful places in nature where it is silent and safe, where I felt free. I usually do something physically active in that context, something that absorbs me and frees me from all other concerns—at least during those connected moments. It is often the simplest, most engaging Highlights that guide us, or sustain us, or give us strength to move through the lowest Lowlights.

## Sustainable Highlights

Sustainable Highlights are usually simple, powerful, uplift-ing experiences. Some may only last a few seconds or min-utes and others may last for hours, days, weeks, or a lifetime. Thousands of different simple connected experiences have the potential to generate good feelings within us and benefi-cial energy gains (Highlights) every day. The duration may be short, but positive, fully connected experiences can con-tinue to lift you and endure over a lifetime.

Sustainable Highlights over your lifetime become a real-istic possibility when you begin to look for and embrace daily Highlights within a number of different experiences or Highlight sources. If you restrict your Highlight choices (or pure connections) to only one source, one activity, or one person, there is a good chance you will miss out on many other Highlight opportunities. One disadvantage of hav-ing only one source of Highlights is that it could disappear: at some point you may no longer be able to participate in that one Highlight activity or pursuit, or that one Highlight person is no longer in your life. It is extremely valuable to have multiple positive Highlight options that can continue to lift you over the course of your life. Diversity in Highlight options and adaptability in finding Highlights in different contexts are great qualities that can sustain a life of High-lights and continue to lift you over your entire lifetime.

The key to ongoing Highlights over the course of your life is to bring a fully connected focus into every little experience or interaction, every day of your life. Simple positive connections every day—with people, activities, nature, and simple pursuits—ultimately bring the greatest ongoing joy and meaning to life. Simple joys live in everyday interactions, experiences, and day-to-day living. Connect fully with simple daily experiences. Be fully there—whether you are speaking with someone, doing something you love to do, trying something new, or responding to an e-mail. Keep your focus open to embrace simple, joyful experiences that can continue to lift you over the course of your lifetime. This is the greatest gift you can give to yourself and others.

Your life of ongoing, sustainable Highlights originates with YOU and the simple choices you make every day. If you sit around waiting for the big win, the lottery prize, or moving to an island paradise, or finding the perfect person or perfect job to start living your life with joy, you may end up waiting a lifetime. That big win, perfect person, or dream goal might well enter your life, and that would be nice. However, even if it does, it will only bring you a life of sustainable joy and meaning if you continue to embrace life's purest and simplest joys every day.

A path with heart is created by lifting your life and filling the lives of others with simple joys. You can begin to walk along this path *right now* by opening yourself to simple Highlights and embracing special moments in each day. Start with the day that you are living right now. Embrace something joyful in small, connected steps as you free yourself to walk along this path. Live each moment that brings connection, meaning, and joyfulness to your life. Remember also that it is often the simplest Highlights that lift you and sustain you through the lowest Lowlights.

You are the captain of your own life. You are the creator of your own story. Choose to live your life now—not in the past, not in the future. Live the way you would prefer to live. Choose to focus on the positives. Choose to find and embrace special moments. Move forward each day with an open heart and fully connected focus.

# 7

# HIGHLIGHT ACTIVITIES

*Highlight activities have the capacity to enhance the lives of everyone on our planet.*

The Highlight Activities in this chapter will help you and anyone important to you to live a more fulfilling life with a greater sense of joy.

## Treasure-Hunting for Highlights

Treasure-hunting for Highlights is a great way to begin teaching children, youth, and adults to focus in more positive and connected ways by embracing life's simplest joys every day. I usually introduce this activity by talking about treasure hunts and then present the idea of going on a treasure hunt for Highlights.

The goal is to see how many simple, happy things (Highlights) you can find while you are on that treasure hunt. I challenge my children to go on a treasure hunt for

Highlights today, tomorrow, or on the weekend. I ask them to remember, write down, draw, or take pictures of happy Highlights they find on their treasure hunt so they can share some of their Highlights with me, other family members, their friends, or classmates.

I have different audio tracks on my Positive Living Skills CD series to introduce specific Positive Living Skills activities to children and youth. For treasure-hunting for Highlights, they listen to "Jessie's Treasure Box" from CD 1 (*Spaghetti Toes*) or "Treasure Hunting for Highlights" from CD 2 (*Changing Channels*). See the Reference section for more information on PLS CDs.

The audio script for "Treasure Hunting for Highlights" is printed below. You can read this script to your children, let them listen to the CD, or simply explain the story in your own way.

> I want to tell you a little story about filling a treasure box with happy things. These happy things are called Highlights. I once knew a girl whose name was Anna. She was not as happy as she wanted to be. She knew she could be happier but she didn't know how to do it. One day I asked Anna if she wanted to go on a treasure hunt for happy Highlights. She said, "I don't know what happy Highlights are, but I once went on a treasure hunt for chocolate candies."
>
> I told Anna that treasure hunting for happy Highlights was different from anything she had done before. To hunt for Highlights, you have to look for all the good things that you can find in your day. Anna said to me, "I really want to go on a treasure hunt for happy Highlights."
>
> When Anna woke up the next morning she said to herself, "Today I am going to really keep my eyes, and my ears, and my heart wide open—to find good things, to do good things, and to feel good things."
>
> This is what Anna told me happened that special day.

"Just after I got up in the morning, my mom came into my room and gave me a big hug." That was the first happy Highlight she put in her treasure box.

"Before I left for school, I ate some pancakes with yummy syrup, which was delicious."

That was her second happy Highlight.

"When I walked out the door of my house I saw a beautiful butterfly . . ."

That was the third happy Highlight she put in her treasure box.

"At school I learned something about dolphins, I finished a painting, and I read a nice story."

Those were happy Highlights 4, 5, and 6.

"At recess, I played with my friends and laughed when we chased each other around."

Those were happy Highlights 7 and 8.

"When I went back into my classroom, I listened closely to a fun story and answered some questions about the story."

Those were Highlights 9 and 10.

"When I left school, I walked to the bus with a friend in my class. When I got off the bus near my house, I looked at some beautiful trees and saw the special color of their leaves. They looked really nice and they smelled good, too."

Those were highlights 11, 12, 13, and 14.

"When I got home, I played outside, then played inside. Then I had a cold glass of milk and two cookies."

Those were happy Highlights 15, 16, 17, 18, and 19, and the day wasn't even over yet!

"At the end of the day before I went to bed, I thought about all the happy Highlights I found to put in my treasure box today. Just thinking about all those good things, and sharing some of them with my family, made me feel very happy and very proud."

The more Anna looked for happy Highlights, the more she found, and every time she found a Highlight, she started to bloom, like a beautiful flower when the sun shines on it. Every day Anna collected new highlights for her treasure box, and every day she grew a little taller, a little nicer, a little stronger, a little more confident, and a lot happier. From the day when Anna went on her first treasure hunt for happy Highlights, she always found something happy in each day. Anna always found good things because she always looked for them and she loved doing it. Whenever Anna went on a treasure hunt for happy Highlights, she kept on blooming like a beautiful flower in the springtime.

Anna told me: "**Hunting for happy Highlights is like going on a treasure hunt every day. The fun thing is that every day, you can fill your treasure box with happy things, good thoughts, and nice feelings. All you have to do is look for the good things that happen each day.**"

Anna wanted me to be sure that I told you to tell all of your friends and all the people in your family: "**Happy Highlights are little things that *you* can find each day. Little things that make you feel good and everyone around you feel good, too.**"

Why don't YOU go on a happy Highlight hunt today, and tomorrow, and the next day? See how many treasures YOU can find.

The ultimate goal of treasure-hunting for Highlights is to learn to look closely and connect fully with something positive in every day, every experience, and every pursuit—no matter where you are, what you are doing, or what challenges you are facing. After you introduce your friends or acquaintances to treasure-hunting for Highlights, invite them to go with you on a treasure hunt for Highlights and see what you can find!

# Look for Highlights

Whatever you are doing, look for Highlights. See how many Highlights you can find when you are listening, learning, interacting, playing, drawing, talking, walking, working, running, riding, reading, resting, or creating something, whether you are at home, at school, at work, on vacation, or on an adventure in the outdoors. Continue to look for Highlights when you are alone, with a friend or group of friends, with classmates, teammates, new acquaintances, or family members. See how many simple Highlights you can find in everything you do, see, experience, or learn today. When participants return from treasure-hunting for Highlights, make sure each of them has an opportunity to share some of their Highlights with others.

## Share Highlights

Sharing Highlights is an excellent way to revisit your own Highlights and expand your Highlight horizon by learning from others. This can be done in pairs, small groups, classes, or meetings—at school, work, or home with family members, friends, classmates, or workmates, at any time, at any place, in any work or social context. Simply share your Highlights with people you know or meet and ask them to share some of their Highlights with you.

What were the best parts of your day today? What were your Highlights this past week or weekend?

The process of sharing good things about your day, your life, and the positive parts of other people's lives is a very uplifting and valuable experience. Exchanging personal Highlights lifts everyone's spirits, creates positive bonds, and opens doors to opportunities for finding new and sustainable Highlights.

## Create Your Own Opportunities for Highlights

Encourage children, youth, and adults with whom you live, interact, or work, or those whom you teach or coach, to create their own positive opportunities for finding Highlights.

Continue to remind those around you—and yourself—to look for and share Highlights every day. Go on a little treasure hunt for Highlights today.

## Connect Fully with Highlights

An experience becomes a Highlight only if you see it, feel it, recognize it, appreciate it, and connect fully with it as a Highlight; otherwise it is just another thing that happens that remains unnoticed or unappreciated during your day. Try to get participants engaged in a discussion on what it feels like to be fully connected with someone or some activity. What does that feel like for you? What does it feel like for different participants in your group? Ask participants to share specific examples of times when they felt most fully connected to something, someone, or some experience. Were you ever so completely connected with what you were doing, seeing, or experiencing that everything else around you disappeared? After they have had an opportunity to share some of their most connected experiences, remind them that this is the best way to fully connect with people and activities for Highlight experiences. "If you want to learn more, perform better, and find more Highlights every day of your life—being fully connected is the way to do it."

## Clicking on Highlights

Clicking on Highlights is a simple and effective way to help children, teenagers, and adults begin to recognize and appreciate more Highlights every day. Ask participants to keep count of how many simple Highlights they can find, or "click on," within a certain time period in any activity or context. They can do this by counting Highlights in their minds when they are engaged in an activity—as was illustrated in "Treasure Hunting for Highlights." Clicking on Highlights is also fun to do with a Highlight Clicker, where you actually click Highlights with a little plastic counter that you hold in your hand.

# My Personal Journey with Clicking Highlights

I am going to share parts of my personal journey with clicking on Highlights to give you a clearer understanding of how I have tried to enhance the quality and depth of Highlights in my own life. The reason for sharing my story is to illustrate one very important point. When we open ourselves to connect fully with each step on our path, there are so many more positive little things that each of us can see, feel, and experience—along any path of life. I have been focusing on connecting with Highlights for most of my life and recently began experimenting with a little plastic Highlight Clicker or Highlight Counter. (You can buy these Highlight Clickers on-line on my Web site, *www.zoneofexcellence.ca* or at *www. gsph.com*. The specific examples presented below illustrate how I have used Highlight Clickers myself and with my children to enrich our experiences with Highlights.

## *Trail-running Highlights*

The first time I took a Highlight Clicker on a run with me, I ran for about sixty minutes and clicked 499 Highlights. This was a very enlightening experience for me because it made me much more aware of the extent to which I experience different ongoing Highlights during my trail runs. I run early in the morning on a natural wooded trail surrounded by trees, alongside a little stream, next to a lake. The winding trail is comprised of lots of different terrains: up hills, down hills, flat sections, bumps, rocks, roots. It became very clear to me on this Highlight Clicker run that I embrace a wide diversity of Highlights during my runs. The sun was shining on my face in different sections of this run. Every time I felt the warmth of the sun on my face, it was a definite ongoing Highlight, every second I felt it. When I ran along next to the little stream, I watched and listened to the water flowing gently, which turned into another series of Highlights.

I experienced many different sustainable sources of Highlights on that run—Nature Highlights, Positive Physical Activity Highlights, Positive Sensation Highlights, Personal Discovery Highlights, Personal Accomplishment Highlights, and at times a sense of pure relaxation. All my Highlights were made possible because I was purely connected with what I was doing, feeling, and experiencing. The special connection with the earth beneath my feet and the natural beauty surrounding me remained a Highlight for me for the whole run. I was also connected with the feeling of my body moving forward fluidly while negotiating different challenges on the trail, the feeling of moving easily and fluidly, the feeling of being able to keep moving forward up hills, on flats, and down hills, the feeling of the sun on my face and cool breeze on my body, the feeling of relaxation through exertion, the feeling of ongoing personal discovery. At some points during my run, I directed my focus to my breathing and this became a sustainable, sequential Highlight. As I breathed out, I clicked a Highlight because it felt so good and easy. My body then breathed in on its own, naturally, which felt good and kept my body going at a steady, smooth pace, which was also a Highlight.

The most revealing part of my first Highlight Clicker run was how easily I could keep clicking the Clicker, because the Highlights were continuous. As long as I remained connected with something positive that I was feeling or doing, I could keep Clicking Highlights. The clearest lesson for me was that when we are fully and purely connected with something, someone, or some experience we like or love, virtually every second can be a Highlight.

## *Skate-skiing Highlights*

On a clear, beautiful, sunny winter day, I went skate skiing (using skis like ice skates) with a friend on a snow-covered frozen lake (without a Highlight Clicker). I experienced thousands of simple Highlights during the ninety-minute adventure, because every stride, every glide, every sparkle on the snow was a Highlight for me. All seven major sources of Highlights were embraced on that one outing, including Positive Human Interaction because I was sharing the experience with a friend and at times we were connected through some very engaging, meaningful conversation. Click, click, click, click . . .

### Running-on-the-beach Highlights

I went for an early morning run on a beautiful, long, sandy beach with the waves rolling up onto the shore. Every wave, every step, every sound, every sight, every smell, every breath was a Highlight for me on that run. Beautiful! Click, click, click . . .

### Massage Highlights

I went for an hour's massage that was given to me as a gift, and every connected second of that experience was a Highlight for me—the touch of strong, experienced hands, the feeling of tension giving way to relaxation in every muscle of my body, the relaxing music, the silent power of a full connection with an experience. Quiet . . . click, click, click . . .

## The Power of Ongoing Connection

Whenever we connect fully and embrace every second of a positive experience—whether it is a massage, a flowing stream, a sunset, physical activity, performance, playing with children, or a connected conversation—it is not just one Highlight. It has the potential to be one Highlight every focused second. Very few Highlight experiences last for just one second. They are often comprised of hundreds or thousands of tiny little Highlights strung together over the duration of a connection, conversation, experience, or event.

## My Children's First Experiences with Clicking Highlights

When I first introduced my children to Highlight Clickers, they were already very familiar with Highlights, having been introduced to Treasure Hunting for Highlights at an early age.

We were sitting at the kitchen table (at suppertime) when I gave each of them a Highlight Clicker. I told them they could use it for clicking Highlights to see how many Highlights they could find in a day. My eight-year-old daughter started clicking right away—first she clicked that I gave her a Highlight Clicker and then gave me a big hug, which she clicked. I gave her a big hug back, which she clicked, and she gave me another hug, which she clicked, and I gave her another hug and laughed, which she clicked, and then she laughed, which she also clicked. She continued to click simple little positive things that made her feel good when she was eating, drinking, playing, drawing, coloring, getting ready for bed, reading in bed, relaxing in bed, and sharing good-night hugs. When she was finally in bed and ready to go to sleep, she had clicked 350 very simple uplifting Highlights.

When I first gave a Highlight Clicker to my eleven-year-old daughter, she was not in her normal happy frame of mind because another child had said something to her that hurt her feelings. I asked her how long she wanted to be upset by this little incident. She took the Highlight Clicker and started clicking—click, click, click, click—a hundred times in rapid succession. She showed me the number 100 on her Clicker, then smiled and said okay, it's gone. She used the Clicker in this situation, not to click Highlights but to help herself change channels from thinking about something negative to something more positive.

## Team Hunting for Highlights

One day when two of my daughters and I were getting ready to go for a nature walk, I asked my daughter Jewelia, who was twelve at the time, if she would bring her Highlight Clicker with her. She graciously agreed to my request. I wanted to see how many Highlights the three of us could find as a team, on our picnic adventure to a flowing stream. Every time any one of us experienced a simple Highlight or series of Highlights, we told Jewelia how many Highlights we had found and she clicked those Highlights on her Clicker. This allowed us to share our personal Highlights as we were experiencing them. It also led to an important discovery. We all discovered that many Highlights continued to be Highlights as long as we stayed connected with them. For example, when we watched the water flowing down a little stream and over a small falls, it turned into an ongoing series of Highlights — as long as we continued to watch, hear, feel, and connect with it.

It was the same stream, but the water flowing over it was different every second. We could choose to continue connecting with different parts of what we were seeing, feeling, hearing, and enjoying if we wanted to. The same was true with walking along the little path through the woods. Each connected step on the crunchy leaves along the meandering trail was slightly different and became a simple Highlight, if we chose to connect. When we sat on a big rock next to the stream, we closed our eyes and felt the warmth of the sun on our faces. This turned into a flowing stream of sunshine Highlights for as long as we continued to stay connected with the feel of the warmth and radiant energy of the sun on our faces.

Our Team Highlight Hunt continued for about eighty minutes — including walking the little trail to the stream, playing in and around the stream, enjoying a little picnic on the rock next to the stream, and walking the trail back from the stream to our starting point. During that time, my daughter clicked 2,473 Team Highlights for the three of us.

Choosing to connect in a positive way in an engaging personal interaction (with one other person) can be viewed in the same way. Each small, fully connected part of that interaction can become a flowing stream of Highlights in its own right.

## Find Your Own Highlights

Focus on finding healthy, life-enhancing activities where you can click on a few happy Highlights or a few hundred or thousand simple little Highlights in a reasonable period of connected time. This will make a huge positive difference in your life. Open yourself and others to opportunities that will free everyone to connect more fully with simple, precious moments. When you make this choice, you move yourself (and your loved ones) from going through the motions of an activity or experience to fully embracing an activity and living your life to the core. This gate is opened by cherishing simple, sustainable Highlights every day, within every possible Source of Highlights.

## Click on Your Own Highlights

Ask the children, teens, or adults with whom you work or live to start clicking on Highlights during different parts of their day. If they have Highlight Clickers, they simply hold the Clicker in their hand and each time they experience a Highlight or anything positive, they click their Clicker (by pushing the button down with their thumb). This keeps track of the number of Highlights they experience over the duration of an activity, interaction, adventure, or day. If they do not have Clickers, participants can simply keep a rough count of Highlights in their heads (or on a pad of paper).

Encourage participants to see how many simple Highlights they can find, remember, or click on during their day. Be sure to give them an opportunity to discuss Clicking on Highlights experiences with other participants. If at the end of the day some Highlight counts are low, is it because there are no Highlights in their day or life, or is it because they are not connecting with the simple joys that are readily available to them? Ask participants to share their suggestions on how everyone can increase the frequency and quality of their Highlights in different activities during their day.

## When to Use Highlight Clickers (HCs)

I have used HCs primarily to increase participants' awareness of Highlights, to get participants focused on Highlights, and to measure changes in the frequency of Highlights over time. Highlight Clickers can open doors for many participants to become more aware of simple joys in any activity, within all of the major sources of Highlights.

People who are highly accomplished at connecting fully and frequently with simple positive experiences usually don't need HCs. However, the HC is still a valuable tool to use periodically as a reminder to continue to look for, and embrace, the simplest joys of your various journeys. If you want to experience sustainable Highlights over time, it is essential to continue to connect fully and joyfully with positive experiences. This usually means finding an effective way to Click on Highlights or potential Highlights—mentally, physically, and emotionally.

## Blinking Highlights

Blinking Highlights is similar to Clicking Highlights, except instead of carrying a Highlight Clicker, you click Highlights by blinking your eyes. When you see or feel a Highlight, you blink your eyes very quickly, similar to clicking a picture with a camera. Blinking Highlights is like taking a mental picture of something positive that you see, do, feel, like, or experience to embrace that special positive moment and hold on to it. Blink, Blink, Blink!

## Breathing Highlights

Breathe in slowly and breathe out slowly for a few easy, relaxed breaths—right now! This is an excellent way to remind yourself to focus on finding simple Highlights every day. Every breath you take is a Highlight because if you stop taking those breaths you lose the gift of life. When you first wake up in the morning, while you are still lying in bed, focus on your breathing. Feel yourself breathe in slowly and breathe out slowly. Remind yourself that you are happy to be breathing and happy to be alive. Then think of one or two positive things that you will do to today to put some joy into this day.

During the day when you are walking, talking, working, reading, playing, exercising, or doing whatever you do, take a moment to check in on your breathing. Focus on feeling your breathing for a few breaths. Remind yourself that you are happy to be breathing—to have the gift of life. Then focus on reconnecting with the step in front of you. Decide to make the best of the moments you are living right now. If you want to focus, remind yourself to do so; and if you need a little break, take one. Focus on your breathing to fully connect or reconnect in positive ways with whatever you want to do, especially when you begin to drift away.

## Highlight Journals

Encourage children, teenagers, and adults to keep a personal *Highlight Journal* where they write down, draw, or insert photos of Highlights, particularly when they are beginning their Highlight Journey. Writing down Highlights at the end of the day, and sharing them with others whenever possible, makes participants reflect in positive ways and remember the good things in their day. They can also revisit those joyful moments any time, simply by looking at their *Highlight Journal*.

**Remind** participants to: record their Highlights in their special *Highlight Journal*, remember their Highlights before they go to sleep at night, and think about some positive things they want to do tomorrow.

## Highlight Games

The following Highlight activities can be used in a variety of settings (at home, school, work, hospitals or treatment centers, activity settings, classrooms, in the outdoors, at conferences or meetings, in social settings) with families, teams, or individuals to help children, teens, and adults find, embrace, and share more positive experiences each day.

## Calling out Highlights

For a certain period of time (for example, during the next half hour or at a birthday party) whenever you, your friends, children, family, teammates, or colleagues experience a Highlight, the person who has a Highlight shouts out, "Highlight!" For example, if I give or get a big hug from you or from one of my children or someone else who is special to me, I say, "Highlight!" They might also shout, "Highlight," assuming that they are playing the game and it is a Highlight for them. Everyone playing the game shouts out Highlights as they occur, or immediately after they experience a Highlight. It's a fun game that most participants enjoy and usually makes everyone smile. It also helps us to remember to look for Highlights and to help others in our presence to find and appreciate more Highlights in their day. If you are all alone at home and feel really good about something you are doing, thinking about, experiencing, or enjoying, you can also shout out "Highlight!" and if you say it loudly enough, I will probably hear you.

## Zing Highlights

Zing Highlights is a fun way of expressing appreciation to another person and also creates opportunities for other people to express their appreciation to you for the positive things you say or do. The guiding light for Zinging Highlights is simple. Whenever anyone says or does anything that makes you feel good, happy, or appreciated, you point at them and make the sound "Zing!" Or you can just smile at that person, look into their eyes and quietly say, "Zing" whenever they say or do anything positive for you or another person. It is also perfectly acceptable to Zing people simply because you are in the same room with them and feel good in their presence. Zing Highlights can be played at almost any age and anywhere at all—at home, school, or any team context; at work, meetings, on holidays—and within all kinds of relationships. It's nice to Zing and be Zinged at least a few times a day.

At the advanced levels, Zing can become like a cooperative ping-pong game, with each player feeding off the positive energy of the other player. I Zing you—you Zing me—I Zing you for Zinging me—you Zing me for Zinging you.

### Highlight rocks

Over the course of a day (or certain parts of the day), participants keep track of their Highlights with the help of Highlight Rocks (or Happy Rocks). Highlight Rocks can be beautiful little polished stones that come in a variety of different shapes and colors, or any kind of small stone that has been washed. If you cannot find rocks or stones, use marbles, dried chickpeas, dried kernels of corn, or anything small and dry that is easy to find. Once the game starts, every time someone discovers or finds a Happy Highlight (something that makes her smile or feel good), she puts one of her Happy Rocks in a bag or bowl. At the end of the game, each participant can see, remember, and possibly share some of the Happy Rock Highlights he or she experienced today. Highlight Rocks gets participants focused on the positives. You are free to start a new game of Happy Rocks—any day.

### Highlight circles

Each participant is given an opportunity to share or act out a personal Highlight within a circle of friends, who try to guess her Highlight.

### Highlight charades

Participants join together in small teams (usually three to six people). First, they each share a Highlight within their team and then together their team chooses one of those Highlights to act out as a team. That means everyone has to play a role in acting it out. They are given a few minutes to discuss and plan their act, and then they act out their chosen Highlight. The other teams that are watching try to guess what it is.

This works equally well with young children, older students, teachers, and business executives at conference workshops.

## Highlight pictures (Show and Tell)

Participants draw, paint, or print a picture of a personal High-light and bring it in to play this game. Each participant then shares his picture and the story behind it with his group, team, or class. Participants can take their own pictures or bring in computer-generated pictures that visually represent their Highlight(s).

## Highlight Pictionary

Participants are divided into several small groups. Within his or her own group, each child draws a Highlight on a chalkboard or on a piece of paper. The other members of their own group look at the drawings and try to guess each person's Highlight.

## Cooperative Highlight egg pass

Participants write or draw a Highlight on a small piece of paper and insert it into a plastic egg (that divides into two halves). You can also use a small envelope or empty match-box. Participants sit in a circle and each time you say "pass," participants pass their egg to the person on their left. When you say "open," one at a time, participants open and share the Highlight inside the egg they are holding. Participants also enjoy trying to guess whose Highlight they found.

## Highlight hunting for similar Highlights

Participants write or draw one highlight on a piece of paper. They then walk around the room trying to find two or three other participants who have the same or a similar Highlight. If they find other participants who have a similar Highlight, they connect and form a group with those people. This game can also be played verbally by participants asking other par-ticipants: "What was your Highlight?"; or silently by point-ing at another participant's Highlight paper, which opens the door to allow her to read it; or by physically acting out a Highlight and asking others to act out theirs.

An alternative to this game is Highlight Hunting for Different Highlights. In this game, participants try to find two or three other participants who have Highlights that are completely different from theirs.

## Wheel of Highlights hunt

The goal of this game is to find and connect with other participants who collectively (together as a group) have recently experienced Highlights in all seven sources on the Wheel of Highlights (Human Interaction, Nature, Relaxation, Personal Discovery, Positive Sensations, Personal Accomplishment, Play / Physical Activity / Sport). Participants are asked to try to find and team up with one or more other participants until their group includes people who collectively have had Highlights (in the past two or three days) representing all seven of the major sources.

## Cooperative Highlight list

Participants put their minds together to think of as many Highlights as they can and write them on a list (within a certain time). This is a cooperative venture and participants are encouraged to add to the list over the course of the day, week, month, or year, as they think of new ones.

## Highlight Jar

Each participant writes or draws a personal Highlight on a small piece of paper and places it in a special Highlight Jar (usually a "see-through" plastic or glass jar). The Highlight Jar remains in the same place in a classroom, home, or eating or meeting room. Participants are encouraged to add to the Jar as they experience new or different Highlights. If a participant is feeling a bit down or wants a reminder of some positive things to do to get a little lift, he or she can visit the Highlight Jar and pull out some Highlights.

## Highlight goals

Participants are asked to set their own goals for increasing the number of simple Highlights they experience and for making sure they find Highlights within the seven different major sources of Highlights. For example, participants can write down, draw, or verbally share the number and type of simple Highlights they *want* to experience today or tomorrow or on the weekend. Then the goal is to go out and find them.

## Highlight Posters

Participants create personalized Highlight Posters with pictures or drawings of positive activities from the Internet, magazines, or their own drawings, writings, or photographs. The posters can be placed on school or classroom walls, at home, or in any other setting where other people can see them.

## Highlight Poster sharing

Each participant can be given an opportunity to share his or her Highlight Poster with classmates, family members, friends, teammates, or workmates. During the sharing process, she/he can talk about the various Highlights depicted in the Highlight Poster and why those activities or experiences are Highlights for him/her.

## Highlight poems

Each participant is given an opportunity to write a poem or story about Highlights or to choose another way to express how he/she feels when he/she experiences Highlights. Participants are asked to share their Highlight stories, poems, or reflections with their family, friends, teammates, or classmates. The following Highlight poem was written by a nine-year-old child who was part of our school-based Positive Living Skills Program. Note that he chose to make the first letter in each word of his poem spell the word HIGHLIGHTS.

**H** appy and good
**I** t's never bad
**G** reat
**H** appiness is the key
**L** ittle things in life
**I** t doesn't have to be big
**G** ood and fun
**H** ave them every day
**T** he good things in life
**S** uper special

# Small Group Highlight Sharing Activities

Sharing positive feelings, experiences, and ideas with other people is a valuable and uplifting experience at all age levels. Here are some simple ways to get participants focused on sharing something positive.

1. Share one thing you like, love, or appreciate about your family, friends, teacher, team, coach, or favorite activity.

2. Share one thing you like, love, or appreciate about a special person or place.

3. Share one thing you like about yourself.

4. Share one thing you did today that made you feel good or happy.

4. Share two Highlights from the past couple of days.

5. Share one positive comment you could make to someone you know well; or do not know at all, for example, a waiter in a restaurant, a salesperson in a store who is helping you, or a new student in school. You might tell him you appreciate something he did or ask him, "What was your Highlight or the best part of your day—so far?"

6. Share one thing you could say or do to get yourself and other people you care about thinking more about positives and less about negatives.

7. Share your ideas with other members of your group to create a new Highlight game. Then try playing the game.

## Create new Highlight games

Encourage children, youth, and adults to create their own Highlight games. Ask them to think of new ways to teach people about Highlights. Get them thinking about how we can encourage more people in the world to live with more harmony and more simple joys.

## Songs of Praise

Songs of Praise are a great way to get people focused on the positives in themselves and in others. These are not singing songs or zinging songs, although they could be if you write a very positive song and sing or zing it. Songs of Praise are sung by people sharing what they feel are some of the best or most appreciated qualities of others. These songs can be shared within almost any relationship, group, activity, circumstance, or context. Here are some specific examples to get you started.

### Sport

I was working with our Olympic basketball team in preparation for the Games. At the final training camp leading into the Atlanta Olympic Games, I met with the entire team (players, coaches, and support staff). I asked a simple question—"What do you like, love, appreciate, value, respect, or admire most about each of your teammates, coaches, and support staff?" I then asked them to write down one or two things they liked or appreciated about each person with colored magic markers, on a large piece of paper, under each person's name. Prior to that meeting, I had taken sheets from a flip chart, written each team member's name on top of the sheets, and pasted them up around the wall with masking tape.

That turned out to be one of the most positive and emotional experiences I had ever seen in a team context. Team members wrote extremely positive and uplifting things about each other. Many of these athletes had never openly shared these kinds of positive feelings with their teammates and support staff before, even though some of those athletes had played together on the National Team for eight or ten years. Members of the support staff also received genuine comments of appreciation that they had never experienced at that level before.

After carefully reading the comments on their own sheets, players went over to other players, thanked them, and hugged them. Some had tears of joy or appreciation. Everyone also walked around the room and read the positive comments that were written about each of their teammates, coaches, and support staff. Overall it was an extremely uplifting and positive experience for everyone. We each took our sheet of positive praise home with us. I still have that sheet of multicolored Highlights with my name at the top and the athletes' positive comments spread throughout the rest of the sheet. It still feels good to read their heartfelt words of appreciation.

## Business

This same Song of Praise activity was extremely well received by employees of a small and very successful local business at a workshop I conducted for them. There were about twenty people in the conference room, from the leaders of the company to the secretaries who keep the company moving forward in positive ways every day. I went through the same process and asked the same question: "What do you like, love, appreciate, value, respect, or admire about each of your teammates, workmates, leaders, and support staff in this room?"

Team members moved around the room writing positive comments under each person's name with magic markers. After everyone had sung their little "song of praise," everyone quickly found the sheet with his/her own name at the top and read it with full focus! They also read the positive comments that were written about all of their teammates. Again there were tears of joy and hugs, with people smiling, laughing, or shaking hands with teammates. It was a very emotional, uplifting, and bonding experience for this business team, similar to the team of Olympic athletes.

## More Songs of Praise

The simple, powerful act of finding and sharing positive things we see in each other (at any age) can be of real value in any context. To begin this process, just ask one or two simple questions: 1. "What do you like, love, appreciate, value, respect, or admire about this person?" 2. "Can you share one specific thing that this person said to you, did for you, did with you, shared with you, or contributed to your life that made you feel good, valued, appreciated, or better about yourself in some positive way?"

When teams of people, families, friends, classmates, workmates, teammates, or new acquaintances begin to look for, find, or share positive things that they like or appreciate in each other, it is of real value for everyone.

You can start singing Songs of Praise in any of the following contexts. Now is a good time to begin. Start with one of these groups this week and then move on to others.

*Family*—Ask each family member to verbally share, write, or draw what they like, love, appreciate, or value about each member of your family.

*Friends*—Ask each of your friends to verbally share or write what they like, love, appreciate, or value about each of their friends.

***Teachers, coaches, students, or study groups***—Ask each of your class members to verbally share, write, or draw what they like, love, appreciate, or value about other members of their class or study group.

***Athletes, performers, or performance groups***—Ask each person in your group to verbally share or write what they like, love, appreciate, or value about each member of their team or group.

***Colleagues or workmates***—Ask each member of your team, group, or sub-team to verbally share or write what they like, love, appreciate, or value about each member of their team or group.

## Close Interpersonal Relationships

One-on-one Personal Songs of Praise are extremely valuable for sustaining or rejuvenating close interpersonal relationships. In this context it is best if both partners in the relationship openly share what they appreciate, like, love, enjoy, value, respect, admire, or cherish about this relationship and their partner in this relationship. This can be done verbally and in writing so the receiving partner can hear it, read it, print it, and hold it in his or her hand and soak in it for a while. It is never too early or too late to begin singing Songs of Praise to important people in your life or to people who previously have had a positive impact on your life. Just try to do it while these people are still alive.

## Personal Songs of Praise

The questions below can be a starting point for Personal Songs of Praise. Adapt the questions to make them appropriate for specific ages, people, relationships, or contexts.

What I like most about you is _____

What you said to me that I liked or appreciated was

_____

What you said to someone else that I liked or appreciated was

_____

What you did for me that I liked is _____

What you did for someone else that I liked was

_____

What I like about the way you are is

_____

What I like most is the way you make me feel good when I am with you.

**Remember**—The most essential rule in singing all songs of praise is to focus only on the positives and not the negatives.

## Sing Your Own Song of Praise

Sometimes we need to sing our own song of praise, especially if no one else is doing this for us. This does not mean that you brag about yourself or act like you are better or more important than other people. It simply means that in the same way that you continue to look for and appreciate positive qualities within others, you continue to look for, appreciate, and nurture the best qualities within yourself.

You can begin this process by answering the following questions.

- What do you like, value, respect, or appreciate about yourself?

- What do you like best about yourself?

- What makes you feel best about yourself?

- What makes you feel best about your life?

- What do you like about the way you are as a human being?

- How would you like to be as a person right now and in the future?

- What can you do to continue becoming this person you want to be on the inside and the outside?

The more demands you have in your life, the more you need to focus on doing positive things to add quality and joy to your life. If you fail to embrace simple joys, you will get caught up in illusions of happiness where there is no substance or no sustainable joy. The fewer meaningful demands you have in your life, the more you need to focus on the good things you do have—simple experiences that bring you the simplest joys. Don't wait until later to embrace simple joys. When you wait too long, many special moments are lost—and they rarely return.

What are some of the best or most treasured Highlight experiences in your life? What were you connected to or feeling during those experiences? Can you create that kind of positive connection again in a similar context or in other contexts—moment by moment, breath by breath, stride by stride, step by step? By gaining a deeper appreciation and understanding of what brings you pure and simple joys, you will empower yourself to embrace more experiences and with greater frequency.

## Choose to Follow Your Own Best Path

- Embrace special moments.
- Open yourself to opportunities.
- Do something that you would really like to do.
- Appreciate simple, connected experiences.
- Feel and express your appreciation to yourself and others.
- Find new Highlights and revisit old ones.
- Share your Highlights with others.

## Follow a Path with Heart

The most powerful Highlights usually come from emotional experiences or connections—where you feel something positive in the core of your being—on an emotional level.

One morning I had a little heart-to-heart conversation with my youngest daughter, Skye, who was eight years old at the time. I spoke with her about the importance of living her life fully and following a path with heart. She asked me, "What is a path with heart?"

I said, "It's a happy path, a positive path, a path that feels good to you, lifts you, and also lifts others. When you are walking along a path with heart, that path feels right for you, and you feel good in your mind, body, heart, and soul."

Later that morning, we went for a walk on a frozen lake that had a thin covering of snow on it—like icing on a cake. She brought a hockey stick with her on our walk. As we moved slowly across the lake, she used her stick to draw a line or path on the snow (similar to dragging a stick on a sandy beach). Every few feet, she stopped and drew a heart along the path. At one point I stopped and asked her, "What are you doing?"

She said, "I am drawing a path with hearts."

I said, "Wow, that's a great idea," and looked closely at every one of her hearts. That path with hearts ended up going across the whole lake. Clicking on Highlights every few feet along your journey is a great way to follow a path with heart—every day of your life.

# FULLY CONNECTED FOCUS

*Every meaningful action, interaction, and personal accomplishment begins with a fully connected focus.*

## What Is a Fully Connected Focus?

A fully connected focus is a complete, positive connection with an experience, learning opportunity, performance, action, or interaction. There is a feeling of being totally absorbed in the experience, becoming the experience, or inseparable from it. Everything else in your life disappears for those fully connected moments in time, and it feels great. Fully focused experiences become possible by connecting mentally, emotionally, and sometimes physically with someone, something, or an experience so completely that nothing else exists for you during that period of time. Your focus is completely connected with what you are doing, seeing, reading, learning, feeling, or experiencing "right now at this very moment."

The goal of a fully connected focus is to experience a sense of total absorption or absolute connection with the moment in which you are engaged right now, and then the next moment, and the next, and the next. A fully connected focus binds you in positive ways with the present moment. Everything negative or irrelevant to what you are engaged in at that moment disappears. During fully connected moments, you are or become more fully alive. This connection might last a few seconds, a few minutes, a few hours, or a lifetime.

# Flowing and Free

A fully connected focus is flowing and free. It flows with you like a stream of clear water and keeps you connected over time—whether you are sitting quietly absorbing the beauty of nature, walking, running, breathing, reading, writing, working, playing, speaking, performing, thinking, listening, reflecting, singing, dancing, or moving mentally or emotionally through a conversation, activity, interaction, or experience.

A fully connected focus is not something that can be perfected or sustained through force or strenuous effort. You free it to work for you by releasing yourself from irrelevant, negative, or distracting thoughts, and connecting fully with what you are doing. When you free your focus to connect fully with an experience, it begins to flow freely, and your life or performance immediately becomes more connected and joyful. This free-flowing connection lives within each of us. You have drawn upon it before and it can continue to sustain you through the ups and downs of your life journey. Free it to surface often in every part of your life.

# Stream of Focus

A fully connected focus in daily living is rarely static or remaining in one place. An example of static focus is staring at a fly on the wall; this can give you an understanding of what it feels like to visually or mentally focus on only one thing. However, in most real-life experiences and challenges, the fly will probably start moving or even fly away.

An effective fully connected focus in most real-world situations is more like a flowing stream of focus that keeps you connected with what you are seeing, feeling, hearing, touching, reading, learning, playing, performing, loving, enjoying, or experiencing. If you focus on following the water in a real stream that is flowing past you, your focus stays with the movement of the water. If you learn to focus *like* a flowing stream, your focus will stay with the movement of whatever you are doing, seeing, feeling, or experiencing.

When you listen with a fully connected focus to someone speak, your focus does not remain centered on only one word. It continues to flow forward as the person speaks. When you are reading a book, such as the one you are reading right now, your focus does not stop with one word and stay there. Your focus keeps flowing in a connected way with the words, sentences, or ideas you are reading or the feelings you are experiencing.

Focus does not stay in the past or in the future for very long unless you take it there—nor does it stay in one specific spot for very long, unless you hold it there. A fully connected focus continues to move forward by staying connected to the present—which is constantly changing every second. In this way, it frees you to continue to absorb or embrace the present moment, image, word, movement, experience, feeling, thought, idea or opportunity. If you are playing a game or engaged in a performance, a fully connected focus frees you to stay focused with the flow of the game, activity, challenge, or pursuit—by keeping you in the present moment.

A flowing stream of focus that keeps you fully connected with each moment of the experience is the most desirable and most fully connected focus for ongoing positive human interaction, learning, performance, and living. Your challenge is to simply—or sometimes not so simply—stay focused with the flow of what you are doing for as long as you can. This is the way to get the best out of yourself and bring out the best in others, every day and in every life context.

## Present Moment—Not Past or Future

A fully connected focus does not dwell on the past or the future. It keeps you centered in the present—even when you are planning a new path or better future.

When you climb a steep hill or a mountain in life that feels like Mount Everest, ultimately you have to lower your head and focus only on the step in front you. This is the only true path to your destination.

## Essential

A fully connected focus is essential for optimal learning, quality performance, and joyful living. It adds joy, meaning, and quality to life. When you open yourself to fully connect your focus, your connection to life will blossom. If you lose or abandon your connected focus, your connection to life and quality in life will begin to dissolve. A fully connected focus is like your breathing or heartbeat— if it stops for too long, your life stops or ceases to be what it can be.

A connected focus can bring immense value to all human life. Anyone can enhance the quality of his or her life by learning to focus in more positive and connected ways. We all can absorb ourselves in our daily experiences, interactions, challenges, and activities. The earlier we begin this lifelong process of full and positive connection, the better.

If we continue to fail to teach our children and youth at an early age to focus in more positive and connected ways in our schools, communities, and homes, we become part of a worldwide human tragedy that wastes huge amounts of human potential, every single day.

## Advantages of a Fully Connected Focus

The greatest advantage of a fully connected focus is the opportunities it creates for living all parts of life more fully. When your focus is fully connected, you learn more, see more, feel more, experience more, remember more, perform closer to your potential, develop more meaningful relation-ships, and live more fully every day. Every positive human action and interaction is enhanced with a fully connected focus—listening, speaking, playing, performing, teaching, learning, working, relaxing, loving, and embracing simple joys every day. Those of us who learn to live our lives with a positive and fully connected focus are more connected, more grounded, and feel more fully alive. When we are physically present in a classroom, gym, home, relationship, social set-ting, or meeting, we have learned to also be fully present mentally and emotionally. A fully connected focus is a dis-tinct advantage for anyone engaged in any worthy pursuit at any age, in any context, at any stage of life.

## Problems Created by a Disconnected Focus

The biggest problem created by a disconnected focus is that it prevents people from living their lives more fully because they are missing out on connecting with so many mean-ingful experiences of potential value. Every positive human action and interaction is put at risk with a disconnected focus. When your focus is disconnected from what you are doing or experiencing, you learn less, see less, feel less, experience less, remember less, contribute less, develop less meaningful relationships, and rarely perform to your full potential. A disconnected focus prevents billions of people from learning what they have the potential to learn, expe-riencing what they have the potential to experience, per-forming to their potential, connecting fully in interpersonal relationships, and becoming what they have the potential to become.

A disconnected focus leads many people to live a hol-low or shallow life, to skim through life on the surface and miss out on many of life's best opportunities. A positive and connected focus helps all of us live our lives to the core by performing and contributing closer to our true potential.

# Personal Connections

What I love best about teaching is when I feel the students are really there, in the moment, with me; I can feel their presence. There is a connected energy in the room that I feel in my heart, mind, and body. I love the feeling of that pure connection when they are sharing their real thoughts and feelings with me and with their classmates or teammates in the room.

What I love best about my one-on-one consulting experiences is that same feeling of pure connection with an athlete, client, or performer. I can feel his or her presence when he/she is really there with me, in the moment, no matter where we are or what is going on around us. There is a connected energy that I feel in my heart, mind, and soul. I love that feeling of a pure two-way connection with them, when they share their real thoughts, feelings, and insights with me and I share mine with them.

What I love best about my writing is the complete and absolute connection I have with what I am thinking, feeling, doing, exploring, and creating through my writing.

What I love about my relationships, sports, speaking, traveling, and moments in nature is the feeling of pure connection with those special people, places, and experiences.

Living your life to the fullest in any context is all about feeling purely connected in positive ways. It's not so much about what you do, it is about the pure connections you continue to make with whatever you are doing or experiencing.

# Discover Your Own
# Most Fully Connected Focus

I have taken the time to discover what a fully connected focus feels like for me and how I can enter that connected place more often. I know that I have the capacity to choose to be fully focused. And so do you! I love the feeling of being fully connected because I know I am really living those moments to the fullest extent possible. Focused experiences make me feel connected, free, and most fully alive. They also leave me feeling calm, peaceful, and glowing, like a quiet lake in the early morning sun. They feel good. They feel right. They feel positive. They connect me and nourish my mind, heart, and soul.

When my focus is most fully connected (for example, when I am writing, running, connecting with nature, or interacting with another human being), I am not thinking about "trying" to be connected. I am simply connecting with the experience and experiencing the connection. When I free myself from other thoughts or concerns, to simply "be here" in the experience, my connected focus surfaces naturally and freely. It never feels forced or effortful.

I love the feeling of being connected and know this connected place is where I prefer to be. I also know that I may not experience a fully connected focus in all situations at all times, but in some contexts I am always fully connected. I know when my focus is fully connected and when it is not fully connected. If my focus drifts, I am usually aware of it drifting away and I can usually bring it back to where I prefer it to be. Sometimes a drifting focus means that I am tired or overloaded or simply need a little break.

I reflect on my best and less-than-best focus experiences every day so I can continue to learn from my experiences and make ongoing improvements in my focus, performance, and quality of life.

## Connected Focus Questions for Reflection

To enhance your own focus, it is important to think about what a fully connected focus feels like and what frees that kind of connection for you. Reflect on why you are fully connected in some situations and not connected in others. Continue to discover what frees you to connect in meaningful ways and to sustain that connection, and what interferes with your most connected focus.

### Most-focused connection

- When is your focus most fully connected (in what situations, activities, or contexts)?

- What frees you to become fully connected?

- What do you feel *during* your most fully connected experiences?

- What do think might free you to remain fully connected for longer periods of time?

### Least-focused connection

- When is your focus least fully connected (in what situations, activities, or contexts)?

- What prevents you from becoming fully connected in those situations?

- What do you feel during your least connected experiences?

- What do you think might free you to become more connected in these kinds of situations?

### Losing and regaining your focus

- If you lose your connected focus, why do you lose it?

- Are you aware of losing it at the time it happens?

- What could help you refocus or reconnect your focus (more quickly)?

### Learning and improving focus

- What can you do to improve your focused connection?

- What can you do to bring your fully focused connection into the different parts of your life?

- What can you do to sustain your focused connection for a longer period of time in different contexts?

# Focus Reminders

The goal of focus reminders is to help yourself or others get mentally ready to connect fully for learning, performing, or interacting—in any context. Once you are engaged in your chosen activity, interaction, or pursuit, your goal is to *stay* connected with whatever you are doing, hearing, learning, feeling, and seeing for the duration of the experience.

Specific, relevant focus reminders can help you and others to attain, improve, or sustain a fully connected focus. Focus reminders are usually key words, images, memories, or best-focus feelings that you can bring with you into different learning, performance, or life contexts. Focus reminders can be used in any situation or context that is important to you. Remind yourself of your best, or preferred, focus, before entering into learning, performance, or relationship contexts and try to respect your best connected focus. This will help you connect more fully and more often, so you can get the best out of yourself, bring out the best in others, and make the best of every opportunity.

# Action Steps
## to Improve Your Connected Focus

If you want to improve your focus, you have to actually *DO something* to make that happen. You cannot just sit there and think about it. Start with the following action steps.

1.  Pick a specific situation that you will be entering soon—where you will be expected to listen, learn, speak, interact, play, enjoy, or perform.

2.  Think about the focus you would prefer to bring into this situation (your preferred focus) and write it down.

3.  Before you enter this specific situation, think about your preferred focus and choose a focus reminder to use in this context.

4. When you enter this specific situation, use your focus reminder (for example, remind yourself to "be here" or recall a previous best-focus feeling that worked for you).

5. When the action or interaction begins in this specific situation, focus only on connecting with what you are doing, or on what will help you do what you want to do. Respect your own preferred focus.

6. When the action or interaction ends in this specific situation, take a few quiet minutes to reflect on the focusing lessons you learned that will help you to continue to improve your connected focus.

   *Answer the following questions:*

   a. What was happening when you were most fully connected (in this context)?

   b. Where was your focus when you were most fully connected?

   c. What was happening when you were least fully connected?

   d. Where was your focus when you were least fully connected?

   e. What lessons can you take from this experience, and act on, to continue to enhance the quality of your focus?

7. Practice using or acting on at least one of the lessons you learned when preparing yourself for a similar context and use it the next time you are in that real situation.

8. Continue to free your connected focus to grow, flow, and blossom in the different parts of your day and life.

9. Smile! You are on a positive path.

# PILLARS OF FOCUS

*We expect people of all ages to know how to focus effectively without ever helping them learn how to focus.*

## Pillars of Focus

Eight Pillars of Focus—Focused Listening, Focused Seeing, Focused Learning, Focused Reading, Focused Playing/Performing, Focused Feeling, Focused Love and Joy, and Focused Reflection—provide a simple framework for teaching children, youth, and adults to become Champions at Focusing. These eight Pillars of Focus can free everyone to learn what they have the potential to learn, perform closer to their capacity, live with more joy and compassion, and become what they have the potential to be. The more Pillars of Focus you have supporting you, the stronger your focus becomes, and the better your life will be.

# EIGHT PILLARS OF FOCUS

When a building is standing on a weak foundation with no solid pillars of support, it can easily crash and fall down, unless we begin to strengthen those pillars of support. When a person is standing on a weak foundation with no strong Pillars of Focus, she or he can easily crash or fall down, unless he or she begins to strengthen those Pillars of Focus. The best way to do this is to begin right now by building and strengthening one Pillar of Focus at a time—one person, one class, one team, one day, one session, one lesson, one experience at a time.

One strong Pillar of Focus is better than none, two are better than one, and so on. The ultimate goal is for all eight Pillars of Focus (or as many Pillars as possible) to become solid, unshakeable assets for you, the people in your life, and everyone in our world. This is accomplished step by step by teaching people of all ages to focus more effectively within each of the key Pillars of Focus that are essential for positive living, effective learning, and performing to capacity in today's world.

When you help people to strengthen one Pillar of Focus at a time, you are providing a great service to them, their community, and our world. Begin with one simple focusing challenge and encourage participants to practice focusing in positive and fully connected ways every day. Even if they focus fully only once a day, that's hundreds of practices in a year. Encourage participants to gradually increase their fully connected focus to five or ten times a day, which turns into thousands of practices and positive focusing experiences every year. The more we practice connecting our focus, the better it gets, and the easier it becomes to focus—in all parts of our lives. As we continue to move along this path of more positive and frequent focused connections, at some point connected focusing becomes a natural part of who we are, how we are, and what we do— just like breathing in and out.

Start by targeting one Pillar of Focus and continue to move forward by helping yourself and others to strengthen that Pillar. Begin with the people you love, teach, train, or coach: family members, colleagues, or anyone else who might benefit from a more fully connected focus. I have provided some simple learning activities below under each of the eight Pillars of Focus to get you started. Once things get rolling, ask your children, students, athletes, performers, family members, friends, teammates, workmates, or colleagues to share or create some of their own ideas for improving each Pillar of Focus. Provide them with ongoing opportunities for creating and sharing new focusing activities and practicing their focus. I am sure they will have lots of good suggestions to keep things moving forward on a positive path.

# Eight Pillars of Focus

1. **Focused Listening**—Listen, Connect, and Remember

2. **Focused Seeing**—Look, See, Connect, and Remember

3. **Focused Learning**—Learn, Connect, and Remember

4. **Focused Playing and Performing**—Play, Perform, Connect, and Remember

5. **Focused Reading**—Read, Connect, and Remember

6. **Focused Feeling**—Feel, Connect, and Remember

7. **Focused Love and Joy**—Love, Enjoy, Connect, and Remember

8. **Focused Reflection**—Reflect, Connect, and Live the Focus Lessons Learned

Focusing is a skill that can be learned, trained, practiced, improved, coached, and perfected like any other skill. When children, youth, and adults are given opportunities to better understand how to focus and then practice focusing every day, and are supported for their efforts, huge improvements can be made. Our collective goal is to teach, encourage, and provide ongoing learning opportunities for all who wish to improve or who can gain from improving their focusing skills. We can begin with the Eight Pillars of Focus.

# 1. Listen, Connect, and Remember

A great deal of human knowledge is transmitted verbally in many different contexts. Listening attentively and remembering relevant information is very important in our world.

## *Listening activities to get you started*

Explain and discuss with children, students, family members, or participants why listening and remembering is important. Then introduce a listening activity where they listen to you or someone else speak about a specific topic (like the importance of listening). Before you ask them to "Listen to Remember," tell them that they will be listening for one or two minutes[1] and then you will ask them to tell you or others in their group what they heard and remember from those one or two minutes. They can also listen to one of my Positive Living Skills CD tracks or a TV or radio interview, story, or song that has a positive message (see Resource section for CDs). The main point is for them to prepare themselves to listen closely, remember as much as they can, and know they will be asked to tell others what they remember from their focused listening exercise. Start with simple stories or topics for short periods of time and gradually increase the length and complexity of the story or content.

---

1    Or whatever time period you desire.

## 2. Look, See, Connect, and Remember

Much human knowledge is transmitted visually through many different contexts. Looking, seeing, watching attentively, and remembering relevant information is very important in our world.

### *Seeing activities to get you started*

Explain and discuss with the children, students, family members, or participants why watching attentively and remembering is important. Then introduce a visual activity where they watch or look for something in the real world (for example, while on a nature walk, in a playground, at a game or performance, or in a shopping mall) or watch a DVD or film clip about a specific topic (for example, from a movie, the Internet, a nature film, or a sporting event). Or ask them to watch a specific series of physical movements that you or someone else does. It can be anything visual—walking; hopping; slow, rhythmical arm, body, or dance movements—that they try to remember and replicate. Before you ask them to "watch and remember," tell them that they will be watching something for thirty to sixty seconds[2] and then you will ask them to tell you and show you or others in their group details about what they saw and remember.

The main point is they plan to focus on seeing and remembering as much as they can so they can tell or show others what they remember from their focused seeing exercise. Start with simple visual images, visual stories, visual experiences, or visual movements for short periods of time and gradually increase the length and/or complexity of the images, stories, or visual content.

## 3. Learn, Connect, and Remember

A huge amount of knowledge, human insight, and perspective is transmitted through learning in a variety of formal

---

2    Or whatever time period you desire.

and informal contexts. Learning and remembering relevant information that is available to you in different contexts of your life is extremely important for your personal development, your children's development, and our world.

### *Learning activities to get you started*

Explain and discuss with the children, students, family members, or participants why learning and remembering something of value from everyday activities, interactions, and opportunities at home, school, and in the community is important. Ask them to choose a specific learning activity or opportunity where they will focus on learning and remembering something of value from that experience. Before you ask them to "Learn and Remember," tell them that they will each select something to really focus on—wherever they are, whatever they are doing (for example, when they are learning something in school, doing homework, studying, practicing, performing, or interacting with another person, their group, friends, or family members). Their goal is to focus fully on their chosen activity and to remember what they learned from that experience. They will then be asked to share with you or their group what they learned and can remember.

The main point is they are to plan to focus fully on learning and remembering as much as they can from the learning activity or context they chose to focus on, and know that they will be asked to share details about what they remember from their focus exercise with you or with their group.

# 4. Play, Perform, Connect, and Remember

Playing and performing provide wonderful opportunities for feeling, experiencing, and nurturing a fully connected focus that can be transferred into many other life contexts. When children, youth, and adults are given opportunities to experience and practice fully connected focusing on a regular basis through their play, sport, physical pursuits, speaking, and performing in a variety of domains, huge positive improvements in focus can be made. Playful or engaging performance activities provide great opportunities to teach, coach, encourage, and highlight the value of a fully connected focus. These activities also open the door to introduce the possibility of bringing this same kind of connected focus into other tasks, assignments, or pursuits, some of which may be less engaging at the beginning but equally important at the end.

An ocean of human passion is experienced and transmitted through playing and performing in many different contexts. Playing joyfully, performing close to capacity, and remembering those positive, connected, uplifting experiences is very important for enhancing the quality of our personal, interpersonal, and global world.

## Playing and performing activities to get you started

Explain and discuss with the children, students, family members, or participants why connecting fully in play and performance is important. Ask them to share why they feel that being fully connected in play, games, sport, and performance might be important. Also ask them why it is important to remember some of those positive experiences. Then introduce a fun game or engaging activity where everyone is included. (See my *Cooperative Games and Sport Book* for suggested games.) Before they begin playing, remind them to "Play, Connect, and Remember" the good feelings. Tell them they will be playing for four or five minutes[3] and then you will ask them to tell you and others in their group details about how they felt while playing, what they were focusing on or connected to, and the good things they remember.

Their goal is to Play, Connect, and Forget everything else while they are playing and to Remember the joy of playing, the connectedness of playing, the good feelings, and the lessons of purely connected play.

---

3    Or whatever time period you desire.

A performance component can also be added to this focusing activity. Pick a performance that everyone is capable of doing to some degree (for example, repeating a simple action or movement, singing a simple song, or repeating a simple positive phrase or statement). Before they begin their "performance," remind them to "Perform, Connect, and Forget" everything else while they are performing and to Remember the Connection, the feeling of being connected or disconnected, and the lessons learned from the experience.

The main point is for them to plan to focus on connecting fully with whatever they are doing or experiencing while they are playing or performing, remember as much as they can about the feeling of their experience, and share possible lessons learned.

# 5. Read, Connect, and Remember

An abundance of human insight, knowledge, and thoughtful perspectives can be accessed through reading books, stories, and other meaningful information in print or on-line. Reading, connecting, and remembering relevant information found in books or personal stories can be a real asset for personal development, child development, and the development of our world.

## *Reading activities to get you started*

Explain and discuss with the children, students, family members, or participants why reading attentively and remembering what you read is important. Then introduce a reading activity where they read part of a book or story. Before you ask them to "Read and Remember," tell them they will be reading a section of a book for two or three minutes[4] and then you will ask them to tell you and/or others in their group details about what they just read and remembered.

Start with reading simple stories or parts of books for a short period of time and gradually increase the length of

---

4    Or whatever time period you desire.

the reading and/or the complexity of the content. This can be done at home, at work, at meetings, or in classrooms at any level—including university classrooms. Participants are asked to read a few assigned pages and share all the details they remember about what they just read. The main point is that they plan to focus fully on reading and remembering as much as they can from whatever they are reading, and know that they will be asked to share details about what they remember with you and their group. This can be easily done in a classroom, family, or work context, where participants are asked to read one page of a book or document and then immediately get together with another person or a small group to share details of what they remember from what they have just read (and possibly how they *feel* about what they have just read).

# 6. Feel, Connect, and Remember

Every human life and every personal experience is touched in profound ways by feelings. Understanding feelings, connecting with feelings, and sharing them is critical to our individual lives, family lives, and interpersonal and global relationships.

Most meaningful human communication that goes beyond the surface is transmitted and acquired through "reading" feelings, "feeling" feelings, being aware of our own feelings, and understanding (or trying to understand or feel) other people's feelings in a variety of situations and contexts. Tuning into and remembering feelings is extremely important for personal development and the future of our communities and our world.

## *Feeling activities to get you started*

Explain and discuss with the children, students, family members, participants, or performers why understanding, expressing, and remembering feelings is important. Then introduce an activity where they choose to focus on their own feelings and remember them in a specific context—for example, when they are in a learning environment, playing, performing, or interacting with other people in school, at home, at work, or in any other context.

For this focusing exercise, let the participants select an activity, interaction, or pursuit that they are already engaged in (for example, when they are alone with friends, classmates, teammates, workmates, or family members), wherever they might be. Their focus goal is simply: "Focus on Feeling what you are feeling in your chosen context. Connect with those feelings and remember them."

If the participants are interacting with another person in their chosen context, they can also try Focusing on Feeling what the *other* person is feeling. "Try to connect with the other person's feelings and remember those feelings." For younger children, you can separate the Feeling Activity into two parts. Today they focus on connecting with their own feelings and remembering them. Tomorrow they focus on connecting with how another person is feeling and remembering *those* feelings.

Before you ask participants to embark upon their "Feel and Remember" assignment, remind them that they will each select one activity or interaction that they engage in (at school, at home, in sport, with friends or family members, in the community, while playing, performing, etc.). They will try to connect fully with what they are feeling in that context during that time frame. If they are interacting with someone else in that context, they can try to also "feel" what that person is feeling. Their goal is to feel and remember what they are feeling, and to feel and remember what someone else is feeling, so they can share those feelings and lessons learned with you and their group. If they are not sure how they are feeling, they can ask themselves: "How am I feeling?" and be honest with their response. If they are not sure how the other person is feeling, they can ask the other person, "How are you feeling?" and ask that person to be honest with his or her response.

The main point is that they plan to focus on being aware of their own feelings and remember their feelings, and they plan to focus on feeling, understanding, respecting, and remembering another person's feelings.

The larger lesson is that it is extremely important to be aware of your own feelings, to understand and feel how other people are feeling, and to draw out positive lessons from those feelings to improve your own life and the lives of others.

# 7. Love, Enjoy, Connect, and Remember

Every human life and every personal experience can be enhanced through love, enjoyment, connection, and remembering positive experiences. Love, connection, and enjoyment are critical to the quality of our individual lives, community lives, and the world at large.

## Love, enjoy, connect, and remember activities to get you started

Explain and discuss with the children, students, family members, participants, or performers why love, enjoyment, connection, and remembering positive experiences are important. Then discuss with them positive, healthy, happy, or uplifting things that they love or enjoy doing.

Ask the participants to pick something positive that they really love to do; for example, sharing connected one-on-one time with a special person—a parent or grandparent, a child or family member, a best friend or any good person whom they really like to be with who lifts their spirits. Simply enjoy some fully connected time with that person or friend—just being together, talking, playing, doing an activity together, going for a walk or hike in the outdoors, or silently enjoying special, connected moments together.

Allow the participants to choose an activity—quiet or active—that they are passionate about or love to do. Ask them to engage themselves in that loved activity alone, with another person, or with a team. It could be any game that they love to play, any activity they love to do, being with any good person they love to be with, or going to any safe place that they love. The simple goal is to choose something positive to do and then *do* it, live it, love it, enjoy it, connect with it, appreciate it, and remember the good parts of it.

The main point is that it is extremely important for you and every other human being on our planet to embrace and nurture love, enjoyment, and positive experiences. It is equally important to remember to share the positive, joyful feelings that become possible through uplifting, life-enhancing experiences.

# 8. Reflect, Connect, and Live the Focus Lessons Learned

Every learning opportunity, performance opportunity, and life experience can be enhanced through personal reflection. For me, this means connecting with the focus lessons learned from reflecting on each experience and acting on those lessons learned.

When anything goes well in any part of your life, there are important lessons you can extract by reflecting on why it went well and what you focused on to make it go well. When very little or nothing goes well, there are equally important lessons you can discover by reflecting on why it did not go well and what you or someone else focused on that prevented things from going well.

It is very important that you stop long enough to reflect clearly and deliberately on your own focus so you can benefit from these essential lessons and continue to act on them. When you begin to reflect and learn from your own focus experiences and live the lessons learned, you become the captain of your own life. You take ownership of your own life because you begin driving your focus in the direction you would prefer to go. This frees you to drive everything that is important to you along a more positive path. This is why ongoing personal reflection, connecting with the focus lessons learned, and acting on those positive lessons is critical to you and everyone else in your life and in the world.

## *Focused reflection activities to get you started*

Explain and discuss with the children, students, family members, participants, or performers why reflecting on their experiences, their best and less-than-best focus, and acting on the focus lessons learned are important. Then introduce an activity where they choose to reflect on a recent personal experience or performance to assess how they were feeling and performing, their focus or lack of focus, and where their focus was when things were going best and less than best.

Ask the participants to select a specific learning activity, performance, interaction, or personal pursuit in which they were involved this past week. For example, they could choose a learning context where they were supposed to be learning something, a performance context where they were hoping to perform their best, a personal interaction context where they were supposed to be connecting in a conversation or interacting in a positive way with another person, or a context where they just wanted to enjoy themselves and relax. This could be something that happened at school, home, work, or within any performance domain or any other context.

Their Focused Reflection goal is to simply reflect honestly on their own focus when things were going best and when things were going less than best. Here are some specific Focused Reflection questions to get them started:

- What were you focusing on, going into this specific learning activity, performance, interaction, place, or context?
- During the activity, when were you most fully connected (or least distracted)?
- What were you focusing on when your focus was most fully connected or helping you most?
- During the activity, when were you least fully connected (or most distracted)?
- What were you focusing on when your focus was least fully connected or most distracted?

- What focusing lessons can you take from this specific experience that can help you to stay focused in a positive and connected way the next time you are in a situation like this?

Continue to reflect on your best and less-than-best focus. Remember your lessons learned and act on them.

The main point is that you encourage participants to continue to assess their best and less-than-best focus in a variety of learning, performance, and interpersonal contexts. Their specific goal is to continue to draw out positive focus lessons and act on those lessons.

The larger lesson is that it is vitally important to become aware of your own focus, to develop a deeper understanding and feeling for how your focus can help you most or how it can hurt you, and to continue to draw out positive lessons from your best and less-than-best focus experiences. Participants should be encouraged to continue to reflect on the focusing lessons learned from their personal interactions and daily experiences (big or small) so they can continue to enhance the quality and joyfulness of each day. This will empower people to continue to improve and enjoy their own lives and the lives of others.

Ask the participants to briefly go through their Focused Reflection questions shortly after every important event, performance, interaction, or experience while it is still fresh in their minds. Give them an opportunity to share their focus reflections and lessons learned with you and their groups.

### *Here is a simple Focused Reflection that YOU can try right now.*

Are you feeling good, uplifted, or happy about your day, or something you did, tried, or experienced today? If yes, what are you feeling good about? What were you focusing on or connecting with when you were feeling good or happy today? What lessons can you learn from having fully focused or fully lived some parts of this day? What can you learn from today to make tomorrow a good, better, or great day?

Are you feeling flat, down, or unhappy about your day or something you experienced or did not experience today? If yes, what are you feeling bad or not good about? What lessons can you learn from not having fully lived this day or parts of this day? What can you learn from today to make tomorrow a more joyful, uplifting, or productive day?

## Benefits of the Eight Pillars of Focus

Relationships, families, teams, classrooms, places of learning, performance, work and play, communities, people, and countries supported by the Eight Strong Pillars of Focus become wonderful places for all people to live, love, learn, grow, and contribute. Strong Pillars of Focus create many new positive possibilities and empower us with essential skills to withstand and overcome many challenges successfully. Pillars of Focus are Pillars of Strength that ground us, connect us, give us more compassion, and nurture our inner strength. We all have the potential to move along this positive path with our own lives, families, children, youth, communities, and world—one person, one Pillar, one connection, one uplifting experience, one positive lesson at a time.

## Final Points

There is one very important point that I feel the need to make clear or drive home with all people in all contexts, at all ages and stages of life. If you are physically there in whatever context you are in, and have the opportunity to learn something, enjoy something, experience something, do something, or contribute something of potential value, you might as well be *fully connected* while you are there; otherwise it is a complete waste of your time and other people's time. Sitting or standing around disconnected, doing nothing, learning nothing, experiencing nothing, enjoying nothing, contributing nothing is a complete waste of time. That wasted time is never returned to you or others; when it is gone, it is gone. So embrace the moment you are living and make the best of it.

One of the great advantages of focusing skills is that you can continue to improve, enhance, and strengthen your focus over the course of your whole life. When you keep using and growing the Eight Pillars of Focus every day of your life, there are no limits. Your focus can continue to grow strength and skill—no matter where or when you start or how young or old you are. As long as you continue to connect fully within the Eight Pillars of Focus and nurture those focusing skills, they will become and remain strong and continue to grow.

## LIVE THE EIGHT POSITIVE PILLARS OF FOCUS

**Focus on Listening**—Remember and Live the Lessons

**Focus on Looking and Seeing**—Remember and Live the Lessons

**Focus on Learning**—Remember and Live the Lessons

**Focus on Playing and Performing**—Remember and Live the Lessons

**Focus on Reading**—Remember and Live the Lessons

**Focus on Feeling**—Remember and Live the Lessons

**Focus on Loving and Enjoying**—Remember and Live the Lessons

**Focus on Reflecting—Live the Lessons Learned**

### REMEMBER TO APPRECIATE

- The good things in your life
- The beauty within you and around you
- The positive lessons you are learning
- The positive parts of your experiences
- The exciting challenges ahead of you

## REMEMBER TO RESPECT

- Your own best focus
- Your own feelings
- Other people's feelings
- How you and others feel when you are connected, supported, and included

## REMEMBER TO CONNECT

and forget everything else when you are playing, living, loving, learning, or performing!

# 10

# FOCUSING ACTIVITIES

*Focusing activities provide opportunities
to teach and nurture fully focused
connections—through practice, training,
and living the lessons learned.*

**O**ne day I was observing young children in an elementary school classroom. The teacher was giving some instructions to her young students. Some children were not listening, so she said to one child, "What did I just say?" The child looked up and replied to the teacher: "I don't know. Weren't you listening either?" This is the way of many attempts to communicate: one person or both are not really listening to what the other person is saying.

# Willful Focusing

Willful focusing is DOciding to focus or "be fully here," wherever you are or whatever you are doing. You choose to connect, listen, see, learn, feel, focus, and remember. You choose to "hear" and remember the most important messages that speaking people or silent people share. You open yourself to create and sustain a focused connection with opportunities that are constantly surfacing or changing—with people, play, learning opportunities, nature, or experiences that touch your heart. Willful focusing becomes possible when you clear your mind from distracting, irrelevant, or negative thoughts and connect fully and joyfully with what you are learning, doing, or experiencing. When you begin to understand and feel that simple, focused connections bring joy, meaning, and value to your life, you open doors to new possibilities.

With practice, willful connected focusing turns into natural connected focusing. You walk into a learning context and you focus; you enter a performance environment and you focus; you walk into a room, you interact with a person or enter a conversation and you focus; you see something beautiful or inspiring in nature or in another person and you focus. It's just what you do.

In the beginning, connected focusing, at least in certain contexts, is driven by choosing to focus, reminding yourself to focus, and learning to improve your focus. In the end, it is not so much about trying to focus—it is more about freeing your focus from other things so you can connect fully and remain fully connected with whatever you are doing.

# The Goal of Focusing Activities

The goal of focusing activities is to improve your focus so you can:

1. Strengthen the Depth of your Focus (create a deeper, more complete connection)

2. Widen the Breadth of Focus (bring your connected focus to a variety of different activities, interactions, contexts, or domains)

3. Extend the Duration of your Focus (sustain your connected focus for longer periods of time)

4. Improve the Quality of your Learning, Performance, and Everyday Interactions and add Joyfulness to every moment of your life

Discuss these four focusing goals with family members, students, participants, friends, workers, or performers when you introduce them to focusing activities. Remind them to keep these goals in mind when they are practicing, performing, learning, or trying to improve their own best focus. When people choose to enhance the depth, breadth, duration, and quality of their own focus, they help themselves and those with whom they live, interact, work, and play to continue along a positive path of focused excellence.

## *Depth of focus*

Focus has many levels: from not being focused at all (like skimming along the surface of a lake or experience), to focused for very limited moments in time, focused some of the time, focused most of the time, to completely absorbed and connected for an entire experience, event, performance, or personal interaction.

Fully connected focusing moves you far beyond the surface of an experience. It takes you to a special place where you connect on a deeper level with an experience, person, performance, interaction, or event. During our most fully connected moments, there is often a feeling of becoming the experience, being inseparable from the experience, or becoming part of the person with whom you are interacting. This feeling of "becoming" the experience is made possible by connecting more fully and feeling the experience on a more intimate level.

## *Breadth of focus*

A fully connected focus has an unlimited range of application; it has no boundaries. It can be applied to everything important in life: learning, playing, performing, working, enjoying nature, interacting, and experiencing simple joys.

Think about the times when you have been most fully focused in your life. What freed this to happen for you? Think about the times when you were not focused at all or focused for very limited moments in time. What prevented you from focusing at these times? How do you think you can expand the depth of your fully connected focus to a wider range of experiences in your life?

## Duration of focus

Focus has the capacity to be either a sprint or an endurance event. A fully connected focus can be sustained for long periods of time in certain contexts; for example, when you are learning, playing, performing, working, engaged in meaningful personal interactions, embracing simple joys, or enjoying parts nature or everyday living. In what parts of your life are you focused for the longest periods of time? What frees this to happen for you? In what parts of your life do you have the most difficulty remaining focused? What prevents you from focusing in those contexts? How do you think you can generate and sustain a fully focused connection for longer periods of time in the different parts of your life?

## Why enhance your focus?

A fully connected focus brings positive human experiences, personal connections, meaningful learning, and all interactions and performances to a higher level. With practice, it is possible and realistic to sustain a high-quality, fully connected focus for longer periods of time in virtually everything you do or experience in your life. When you immerse yourself and others in the art and practice of connected focusing, you become your own greatest asset and cease to be an obstacle to your own learning, living, and performing. The ultimate goal of teaching and practicing a fully connected focus is to live a more joyful and meaningful life and to help others to move themselves forward along the same positive path. These are the many good reasons for you and others to practice enhancing the depth, breadth, and duration of focused connections—every day.

# An Inside View of Focus

## *Outside-in focus*

This is when an outside experience grabs your focus and pulls you in. Sometimes it doesn't require practice, a willful intent, or focus reminders because the outside stimulus is so strong that it pulls you in quickly and easily, and the connection feels natural. Basically the outside comes into you and you let it in—simply by opening your eyes or ears or heart. A clear example of an Outside-in Focus is watching a really gripping movie or a skilled performance or reading a riveting book. Every scene, page, or image can be captivating and take you to a connected place—mentally, physically, or emotionally. You may be sitting in a theatre, stadium, or arena with hundreds or thousands of other people, or sitting in a crowded waiting area reading a book, but mentally and emotionally you have entered a different world because you are fully connected with another world of experience. Creative writers, artists, film makers, actors, and other skilled performers devote tens of thousands of hours and many years to sustain their own focus—and hold your attention for an hour or two. There is great power in a fully connected focus. It can take you places you could otherwise never go.

Clearly, not everything of value that we can benefit from learning, doing, improving, experiencing, or contributing in our lives is as exciting or easily absorbing as watching a great movie, seeing an amazing performance, hearing an inspiring story, or reading a riveting book. Fortunately, we have the capacity to learn and to become fully connected in a wide variety of other daily experiences, interactions, and learning and performance contexts. Initially we may connect for only short periods of time, but with practice, we can develop the skills to maintain our focus for longer periods of time, within a variety of different contexts. This includes school, sport, music, drama, dance, personal interactions, nature, work, and every other human learning and performance domain. A fully connected focus is a realistic goal to attain and sustain in virtually any meaningful life context.

You just have to open the door to connect and then practice the art of fully connected focusing.

## Inside-out focus

This is when you generate a focused connection on your own, from the inside out, by directing your focus to connect with something outside of you. The reality of daily living, learning, and performing is that not all outside experiences or learning or performance opportunities come jumping out at you or into you. You have to jump into them, connect with them, learn from them and benefit from them. In the beginning, it can be challenging to generate and sustain an Inside-out Focus because this focus comes totally from within you. You have to make this focused connection happen and sustain this connection. No one can do it for you.

Your personal Inside-out Focus is probably the most important learning focus in your life, because it creates real possibilities for ongoing learning, performing to your capacity, positive personal interactions, and joyful living—every day.

An Inside-out Focus is like an energy beam that lives inside of you that you can radiate out to make a connection with something or someone of value (or potential value) outside of you. When you get your Inside-out Focus working for you, it generates an easy, natural, and pure connection with whatever you are doing or experiencing. It is a sustainable focus because what you are seeing, doing, learning, or experiencing can keep changing in some way every day, and what you are connecting with has the potential to make a real difference in your own life and the lives of others.

## Inside-in focus

This is when you create a focused connection with a feeling inside of you. You accomplish this by directing or beaming your focus to connect with this feeling that is living within you. It could be a physical feeling in your body, an emotional feeling, a feeling of joy, a best-performance feeling, a best-connection feeling, or a gut feeling or intuition.

An Inside-in focus allows you to connect with your own unfiltered feelings—to feel your true feelings, learn from them, and benefit from them. Your Inside-in focus is probably the most honest and intimate human connection because it is directed totally within and comes totally from within you. It allows you to be completely honest with yourself, to feel or explore what you are really feeling and begin to understand what you are feeling. It also helps you to choose, guide, respect, and follow your own best path.

## Focusing Activities to Get You Started

Every focusing opportunity, experience, pursuit, and lesson learned in life has the capacity to enhance living, learning, loving, and skilled performance. It is advantageous to begin teaching focusing skills to children and youth so they can learn to connect and sustain their focus in positive ways early in life. We clearly have the capacity and tools to teach children and people of all ages focusing skills that will help them to bring the best out of themselves and others. Let's begin right now with some of the following focusing activities and continue to move forward from there. The earlier we begin this process, the better for everyone.

The purpose of focusing activities is to engage participants in simple daily opportunities where they can practice focusing and to help them feel a fully focused connection within a short period of time. The focus goal is to help them to learn to connect fully with every meaningful experience or activity they are involved in. Every time we experience a fully focused connection and remember what it feels like, we gain a better understanding and feel for what our best focus is and how we can create and sustain that focused connection. The long-term focusing goal is to continue to extend the frequency, depth, and duration of their fully focused connection in different contexts of their life, so they can give and get the best out of their time, opportunities, and life experiences.

The following Focusing activities were designed to help you and others practice and strengthen simple, positive, connected focusing. These activities and games will get you started. You, your children, students, performers, colleagues, and others can then begin to create your own activities and games for enhancing and sustaining a fully focused connection. Once you start moving along this path of focused excellence, it is very easy to find additional ways to practice focusing—because almost everything we do, see, or experience in life can be turned into a focusing activity or game. Focused excellence is a self-directed process. Others can help you or guide your focus, but in the end you are the only one who can direct and sustain your focus. No one can jump inside your brain and do that for you. You are the boss of yourself and your focus. Make it your strength and direct it wisely.

# What Is Focus?
# A Lead-in to Focusing Activities

I often begin focusing activity sessions by asking children, youth, and adults the question: "What is focus? What is focus for you? What does being focused mean to you?" I go around the group asking each participant to briefly answer this question in a sentence or two. Even young children (six- and seven-year-olds) have some very interesting and valuable ideas on what focus is ("just doing what you are doing when you are doing it") and what focus is not ("not talking"; "not thinking about other things"; "not doing other things when you are trying to do this thing"; "not doing other things in your mind or bothering others when you are supposed to be listening").

When people of all ages share their views or understanding of focus, I thank each of them for sharing. I am very respectful of their views and appreciative of their willingness to share with me and their group. I also share my own views and tell them that "focusing is very important—in everything you do right now and everything you will ever do in your life: learning, performing, doing good things you want to do, helping others, having good friends, and having fun. That's why it is important to make our focus as good as it can be!"

# Seeing Activities

A great deal of communication, knowledge, and understanding is transmitted visually in many different contexts. Seeing clearly, observing attentively, and remembering relevant images and information is very important in education, relationships, work, performance, and positive living in our world. Explain and discuss with students, family members, or participants why seeing and remembering is important. Then introduce a focusing activity where they have to look at something very closely and remember tiny details of what it looked like. Before you ask them to "see and remember," tell them that they will be looking at a small object (for one or two minutes) and then you will ask them to remember exactly what they saw.

## *Focus on sticks*

When I first introduce a focusing activity, I tell the participants that the focusing activities we are going to do can help us all learn to get better at focusing in everything we do. I then introduce a simple focusing activity—like focusing on a little stick—to give them a tangible experience with focusing right away. I begin by giving each participant a small twig (or other simple small object to focus on—a leaf, small rock, or piece of dry cereal). I ask them to really focus on that stick (or other small object) so they get to know every part of it. I say, "See it, touch it, feel it with your fingers. Look at the littlest parts of it, bumps, shapes, dots, designs. Get to know your stick [or whatever the participant is looking at] by focusing fully on it and nothing else.

"For the next minute (sixty seconds) we are each going to really focus on our own little stick. The only important thing for the next sixty seconds is just you focusing on your little stick. Nothing else matters. So really focus on your stick—get to know your stick."

I also tell them that after that one minute, I will collect their sticks, mix them all up, and then everyone will focus on trying to find their own unique stick. Before they put their little stick into a pile with the other sticks, I remind them to: "Look at your stick very closely one more time—focus on your stick so you can find YOUR stick when it is mixed with other sticks. Focus on seeing, connecting, and remembering your stick."

I start with groups of five or six children (or adults) when first mixing their sticks (or objects) together so their chances of finding their own stick is higher. If they are successful at finding their own stick, I ask them to share how they found it or how they knew it was theirs. This gets them sharing specific aspects of what they focused on and how they remembered their particular object. Then I ask them to focus on their own stick again, because we will now be mixing their sticks with a larger group of sticks, and again they will focus on trying to find their own stick. They are usually successful at finding their own object; if someone cannot find his or her stick, others help to make sure everyone finds theirs. Adapt the difficulty of the focusing challenge to the level of the group and continue to increase the focusing challenge as they become more skilled at focusing.

The last time I played Focus on Sticks was with a diverse multicultural group of six- and seven-year-olds. They really enjoyed the activity and I really enjoyed playing with them. At the end of the activity session, they all wanted to keep their special stick and take it home with them. I asked one little boy, "Are you going to keep your stick?" He responded excitedly with two words: "Yes, forever!"

### Focus on leaves, stones, pieces of dry cereal

This activity is similar to focus on sticks except the participants focus on different objects. It can be played with any kind of dry cereal (Cheerios, Rice Krispies, Corn Flakes, etc), leaves fallen from any kind of tree or bush, small stones, pebbles, rocks, dried chickpeas, kernels of corn, acorns, flowers, ferns, dried sea shells, blades of grass, nuts, peanuts in their shells, dried seeds (pumpkin, melon, or watermelon seeds), small candies, any fruit or vegetable (carrots, apples, coconuts)—or anything else that is small enough and safe enough to hold in your hands. At first glance they all look the same, but with a more focused connection, each is uniquely different. This is a simple and fun focusing game to begin with for people of all ages.

The procedure is always the same: Give each participant an object to focus on. Ask the group to focus on looking very closely at the unique object they have in their hands—because later they will have to find their own leaf, Corn Flake, or small stone, when it has been mixed together with all the other leaves, Corn Flakes, or small stones. Give the participants a minute or two to really focus on their own leaf, flake, or stone. Then ask them to get into groups of five or six, gently mix up their leaves, flakes, or stones, and see if they can find their own unique object. If they find their own object in the small group, ask them to form larger groups, and mix up their leaves, flakes, or stones—and see if they can find their own unique object in the bigger group.

When all (or almost all) participants have found their unique objects, ask them how they were able to do it. What did you focus on to find your own unique leaf? When were you most fully focused on your leaf, flake, or stone? What did it feel like to focus like that? Were you aware of anything else or thinking about anything else when you were most fully focused on your object? How did you get yourself to focus like that? Do you think you can bring your "leaf focus" into other things you are doing?

How are you going to remember to do that?

## *Focus on everyday miracles*

Focus on a sunrise, sunset, or cloud in the sky. Continue to watch how that sunrise, sunset, or cloud moves or transforms. Focus on a star, the moon, a raindrop, a tree, or a flower. Focus on walking, talking, smiling, skipping, running, playing, or holding onto a hug (not a bug) for at least ten seconds. Focus on listening, caring, sharing, helping, or making someone feel good, accepted, happy, or important.

## *Places to find objects for focusing games*

If you live near a Dollar Store, go to the crafts area. You can find bags or boxes of small objects (sticks, small slices of wood, shells, stones, dried fruits, nuts, and so on) that are inexpensive and perfect for doing simple focusing exercises. If you live near an outdoor setting (a forest, bush, woods, beach, lake, or ocean), you can pick up lots of interesting objects to focus on such as leaves, blades of grass, small stones, or shells that are lying on the ground or sand. You can also ask children, teens, or adults for their suggestions for good objects to focus on for this game. In one class, the children decided to all draw a happy face on pieces of paper that were all the same size and color. They mixed up their happy faces and focused on finding their own happy face and tried to guess who drew other happy faces.

### Eye connection

This is a focusing game that begins with eye contact. Players form a circle, stretch their arms out to their sides so they can touch fingertips with the person on each side, and then drop their arms. The goal of the game is to make eye contact with anyone in the circle and then say something positive to that person. As soon as two players "meet" with their eyes, they walk toward one another, shake hands, exchange greetings ("Hi, I'm Terry"; "Hi, I'm Laura"), exchange positive comments ("I like your hat, Laura"; "I like your smile, Terry"), and look into the other person's eyes as they thank each other ("Thanks, Terry"; "Thanks, Laura"). Then players immediately try to make mutual eye contact with another person. Many positive exchanges can occur at the same time and within the same game when players focus on making eye contact. Positive comments can include anything that will be received in a positive way (e.g., I like your eyes, hair, shirt, voice, shoes, energy, the way you treat others, or any other personal quality).

## Listening Activities

### Listening and remembering

A great deal of human communication, understanding, and knowledge is transmitted verbally in many different contexts.

Listening attentively and remembering relevant information is very important in education, relationships, work, performance settings, and daily living. Explain and discuss with students, participants, family, or team members why listening and remembering is important. Then introduce a listening activity where they listen to you or someone else speaking about a specific topic. Before you ask them to "listen to remember," tell them that they will be listening to something for one or two minutes and then you will ask them to tell you and others in their group what they heard and remember from those few minutes.

This listening and remembering activity can also be done with any of my Positive Living Skills CD tracks, a radio or TV interview, a song, or a story that has a positive message. The main goal in listening activities is that participants choose to listen closely, remember as much as they can, and know they will be asked to tell others what they remember from their focused listening exercise. Start with simple stories, CD tracks, or interesting topics for short periods of time and gradually increase the length and complexity of the story or content. All my Positive Living Skills and Zone of Excellence CDs can be used as focused listening activities (see Resource section).

## *Clicking in and checking out*

When your goal is to help people learn to listen, learn, and connect more attentively, the game of **Clicking In** can be helpful. Remind participants to **Click In** to Listening before you start talking or before they enter a conversation or learning context. Remind them to remind themselves to **Click back In** if they are starting to drift away or are checking out when they are in a learning or performance context, classroom, or conversation.

Ask yourself: Are you honestly checked in on listening right now? Are you really connecting with the person who is speaking (teacher, coach, friend, partner, child, parent, colleague)? If you are really checked in or **Clicked In** — Great! If you have checked out, try **Clicking In** again. When you are trying to learn something or improve something, or you are interacting with a person or friend who wants you to listen, why not listen? Are you doing something more important or more valuable when you sit or stand without listening?

When someone says to you, "You are not listening!" they are usually right—even when you say, "Yes, I am listening!" To make sure you are listening, check in with yourself. If you are not listening, simply say, "I'm sorry" and Focus Fully on Listening to what that person is saying, sharing, or feeling. **Click In** to Listening. This will help you learn more and make other people feel better.

If someone is not really listening to you, sometimes you can tell by his body language (for example, he is not looking at you or he is focusing on other things while you are speaking). It is not a good feeling when someone does this to you because it makes you feel like he doesn't care about you, or respect you, or value what you have to share.

If you check in with yourself and you know you are not listening, **Click In** to Listening. And if someone is not listening to you, tell her you would appreciate it if she would **Click In** and Listen to you, because there is something that you would like to share with her.

Fully connected listening is one of the most important ways of showing another person that you value, respect, and care about him and value what he has to say. It is one of the best ways to understand and nurture a positive relationship with another person. Listen to his words . . . tone of voice . . . feelings. Practice doing this every day. Fully connected listening is one of the best ways to learn, know, understand, and remember, and to open yourself to stretch your mind to new positive possibilities. Really *listen*!

### Listening and not listening

This listening activity helps participants experience what it feels like when someone does not listen to you and when you do not listen to her. In this game, partners sit facing each other in chairs or on the floor. Anna is asked to tell Joey what she did on the weekend (or what her favorite activities are). Joey is told to listen for a sentence or two and then pick up a magazine, book, or newspaper (which would be lying on the floor next to him) and start reading it while Anna is still talking.

After about fifteen seconds of not listening, everyone is asked to freeze—to stop what they are doing. Anna then tells Joey what she felt when Joey picked up the magazine and started reading while she was talking. (Joey can also share how he felt, picking up the magazine and ignoring Anna.) Partners then switch roles to observe what it feels like to be the person ignored and the person doing the ignoring.

Partners can then repeat the listening exercise—showing great interest in what their partner is sharing, for example with eye contact, leaning forward to really listen, making a positive comment ("Cool!") and asking for more details about what she or he did on the weekend. Then let them discuss how this felt for each of them.

## Circle of friends

Each person teams up with another person, either an old friend whom they already know or someone they do not know. If Doug does not already know his partner's name, first he asks Adam his name. Then Doug asks his partner Adam to share something he really likes or loves doing. The listening goal is to focus on listening closely to hear and remember the partner's name and to remember what the partner likes or loves to do. All partners then sit next to each other in a circle so they can each introduce their friend to the rest of the group. For example, I say, this is my friend Maria (and I raise her hand in the air): she likes dancing and ice cream. And she says, this is my friend Terry (and she raises my hand in the air): he likes smiling and running. All the other partners in the circle then introduce their friends in the same way. Focused Circle of Friends can also be played by asking partners to share something positive they like or appreciate about their friend. This activity gets everyone focused on finding something their friend likes and finding something they like about their friends. It also encourages listening and the sharing of positive qualities and experiences with others.

### *Sound connection*

This is an active focusing game where participants have fun focusing on listening through many distractions. A large group, team, or class is divided into smaller groups with about five people in each group. Each group of five joins together in a circle and decides on a team name or animal sound (for example, a wolf howl) that they can use to "call" their group together with their eyes closed. All members of all teams then spread themselves around the room or play space. They all close their eyes, turn themselves around three times in a circle, and try to reconnect with all members of their team (with their eyes closed), communicating only by calling out their animal sound or team name. Each team member focuses on calling out his or her sound and listening closely for the special sound (or howl) called out by his or her teammates. This continues until all the team members are back together in their original groups. This is a really fun game to play and to watch when other people are playing. Younger children (and even some struggling adults) are allowed a peek or two if they cannot find a team member.

### *Focus on listening to voices*

With open eyes, each person in the group shares one thing he or she likes about a family member or friend, while others in the group focus on listening closely to that person's voice to hear and remember what she or he is saying and what his or her voice sounds like. Then they all close their eyes and listen to the same voices sharing the same things they like about a family member or friend and try to guess (or open their eyes and point) at the person who just shared a positive thing. Start in small groups and gradually build into larger groups. Ask the participants if they focus on listening to other people (family, friends, teachers, coaches, colleagues, new acquaintances) in this same fully connected way.

### *Song focus*

Pick a song that has a positive message for participants to listen to, preferably a song that has words (or lyrics) that they have not listened to in a focused way before. Ask them to listen closely to the words and the message of the song, so they remember and share the words and message with other members of their group.

## Listen to learn focus

Listen to your teacher, coach, parent, partner, or friend in a fully connected way today. Listen with a willful intent to:

1. Connect fully with what is being said

2. Remember what is being said

3. Act on the most important point that is being said (or not said)

When you connect fully within any experience, remember that connected feeling and choose to bring it into other things you do.

## Focus on the sounds of nature

Go to a place where birds are chirping or singing, trees and leaves are making music when there is a breeze, water is flowing, waves are caressing the shore, or there are other sounds, smells, or feelings of nature. Sit, stand, or lie down in silence, listening to all the sounds you can hear in a natural setting. If you can't go to a place in nature, listen to a CD that has nature sounds—see how many different kinds of sounds you can hear (wind, waves, birds, animals, etc.). Then share the sounds and feelings you remember.

# Feeling Activities

A great deal of joy and understanding that goes beyond the surface is transmitted through feelings in many different contexts. Opening yourself to feel, embrace, and remember feelings—especially good feelings—is very important in relationships, learning, understanding, work, performances, and joyful living. Explain and discuss with students, family members, or participants why connecting with feelings and remembering good feelings is important. Then introduce a focusing activity where they have to connect with good feelings and remember those good feelings. Connecting with Feelings is an important part of Listening, Seeing, Learning, Performing, and Living.

## Focus on feeling the sun on your face

Go outside on a sunny day and find a quiet place (if possible). Sit or lie down and close your eyes with your face facing directly at the sun. Focus on the feeling—and connecting with that feeling—of the sun radiating warmth and light on your face. Try to sustain that feeling of pure connection with the sun; try to keep feeling it—like a flowing stream of sunshine that continues to bring warmth and positive energy to your face and your body. Just connect with that feeling and nothing else.

## Focus on feeling the wind on your face or body

Sit or stand outside in a safe place when the wind is blowing. Close your eyes, stretch your arms out to your sides, and focus on feeling the wind on your face and body. Focus on feeling how the wind is making contact with you: Where do you feel it? What does it feel like? Is the wind changing? Is it touching you in different ways or on different parts of your face or body? Once you feel the connection with the wind, open yourself to sustain that fully connected focus by continuing to feel the cooling or awakening touch of that ongoing flowing stream of wind.

## Focus on your breathing

Sit, stand, or lie down and focus on your breathing. As you breathe in slowly, listen to the sound of the air entering your body—and feel the air going into your body. As you breathe out slowly, listen to the sound of the air leaving your body. Feel the air leaving your body. As you breathe in, imagine that the air you are breathing in is filling your body with positive energy. As you breathe out, feel your whole body relaxing. Continue to breathe in and out slowly and continue to connect with the sound and feeling of your breathing.

## Focus on listening to people's feelings

Listen to a person with an open mind and open heart. Listen with your feelings. When you listen with your feelings, you begin to understand what is really being said and what is not being said. Open yourself to focus on feeling what this person is really saying or what she or he is trying or crying to communicate. Listen to the feelings behind or beyond the words. When you "listen" in this way to children, teenagers, parents, teachers, friends, partners, or teammates, it makes them feel valued and understood. This is Fully Connected Listening.

## Focus on listening to your own feelings

Listen to your own feelings—your honest feelings. When you stop and listen to your own feelings with an open mind and open heart, you begin to understand how you are really feeling. If you can't always be honest in sharing your feelings with others, at least be honest with yourself. This can help you make good choices and guide you along a path with heart. If you have a trusted person in your life who will listen without making judgments, consider sharing some of your feelings with him or her.

## Connect fully with one person today

Really connect with one person you see, meet, or speak with today—be totally connected and not thinking about anything or anyone else. Live and feel those fully connected moments, learn from them, and remember what they feel like.

## Connect fully with one experience today

You live this experience, this moment, only once—then it is gone forever. So choose to live and feel this one experience in a fully connected way today.

## Reeling in good feelings

Sometimes when I have my best days, I feel like I am "reeling in" good feelings, no matter what I am doing or what direction I am moving in. I cast out my focus and see how many good feelings I can reel in. Try it! See if it works for you.

## *Reeling in good feelings in physical activities*

Sometimes when I am running, I feel like I am casting out a fishing line and constantly reeling in good feelings in front of me—on the trail, up the trail, beside the trail. I am reeling in the hills and the Highlights. Occasionally, my reeling-in hand actually starts turning like I am actually reeling in all these good things. I don't actually have a fishing rod in my hand, but the image of reeling in good things, good feelings, and positive little accomplishments along my path is real and feels real. Some distance runners talk about "reeling in" a person—or a mile marker, tree, or telephone pole—in front of them. What I do feels a bit like that, but I am often alone on my trail and I am reeling in the hill and other good things in my life and along my path. I always have good feelings about that and carry those good feelings with me.

# Focusing in Different Contexts

## *Be Here*

The most important part of learning, performing, and interacting in any context is learning and perfecting the skill of "Being Here." To focus most effectively in any context, you have to be totally "here" in this moment when you are here, and fully focused in the next moment when you are there. **Be Here** is a simple focusing activity designed to help participants practice bringing their focus into the present moment and keeping it there. You can play **Be Here** anytime, anywhere, in any context, for example, while you are doing focusing activities, playing, listening, doing homework, studying, practicing, looking at someone, seeing beyond the surface of something, walking, running, sitting, standing, talking on the phone, working, getting ready for a performance, or performing.

   ***Rules of the game***: while you are engaged in a learning activity, interaction, performance, or pursuit, repeat to yourself in your mind (or out loud if necessary), "**Be Here, Be**

**Here, Be Here**" in a rhythmical sequence three times in a row. And if your focus drifts away, repeat "**Be Here, Be Here, Be Here**" in a rhythmical sequence five times in a row.

## Be Here (combined with breathing)

**Version 1:** Repeat "**Be Here**" in a rhythmical way with your breathing.

Breathe in slowly and say to yourself "**Be**" as you are breathing in. Then as you breathe out slowly, you say to yourself, "**Here**." Try it yourself right now—with your breathing. Breathe in . . . **Beeeeeeeee**. Breathe out . . . **Heeeeeeeere**. Breathe in . . . **Beeeeeeeee**. Breathe out . . . **Heeeeeeeere**. Good!

**Version 2:** Repeat "**Be Here**" in a rhythmical way with your breathing.

Breathe in slowly and say to yourself, "**Be Here**" as you are breathing in. Then as you breathe out slowly, say to yourself, "**Be Here**." Try it yourself right now—with your breathing.

Breathe in . . . **Be Here**. Breathe out . . . **Be Here**. Breathe in . . . **Be Here**. Breathe out . . . **Be Here**. Good!

"**Be Here**" combined with breathing also works very well when you are in learning or performance contexts and when doing something physically active. Participants can be encouraged to discover their own best ways to remind themselves to "**Be Here**" in different contexts and share their best discoveries with teammates, classmates, workmates, or others.

## Free Here

**Free Here** is similar to **Be Here**, except you use "**Free Here**" as a reminder instead of "**Be Here**." **Free Here** reminds you that you are Free to Be Here and Free to get the most out of Being Here. When you repeat "**Free Here**" five times in a row, it usually serves as an effective reminder to free yourself to be fully connected here in this moment. Once you are connected in the moment, the goal is to stay **Free Here** for as long as possible. If you begin to drift away, repeat "**Free Here**" in rhythm with your breathing.

## *Focusing in games*

Many children and youth can focus more readily in games, sports, and other physical activities, because there is something clear, specific, and urgent (but not really urgent) to focus on: running after a ball, kicking a ball, batting, catching, shooting, putting, skipping, skating, jumping, running, diving, climbing, swinging; or playing active games, board games, card games, pretend games, or focusing games. Focusing activities that are active, fun, and engaging help children, youth, and adults to sharpen their understanding of what it feels like to be fully focused. They also give participants lots of opportunities to practice improving their focusing skills. The performing arts (acting, dancing, making music, singing, etc.) and visual arts (drawing, painting, sculpting, pottery-throwing, etc.) also provide great opportunities to feel, practice, and refine fully connected focusing skills.

## *Focusing in everyday contexts*

Effective learning, performing to capacity, and engaging in uplifting, meaningful interactions require a fully connected focus. However, not all learning contexts, personal interactions, and performance pursuits are as naturally engaging as playing games or sports or engaging in some other joyful activity. For example, many people may not be that excited about listening to someone speak, or listening to instructions, following instructions, reading assignments, doing homework, or learning something "important" that to them is not very exciting or "important." However, if we are able to get those people focused or engaged in learning, they will almost always find value in what they are learning and how they are learning. This is why it is so important to teach all children and youth how to focus for learning and ongoing improvement (in all educational contexts and outside those contexts). This can begin with a discussion on what a connected focus is, what it feels like, and why it is important. Participants can share examples of times when they have been most fully focused on something they have done.

If a person at any age has a vivid memory of connecting fully in any context (physical challenges, music, drama, singing, playing games, speaking, listening, reading, helping someone, interacting with a friend or favorite animal), we know she is capable of focusing in other contexts. We can ask her to talk about those vivid experiences or memories of a fully connected focus in any context. We can challenge her to focus that way in different learning or performance contexts—even if it is only for a very short period of time. We can encourage her to gradually extend the time for which she can maintain that fully connected focus in different learning, performance, or personal interaction contexts.

We can remind her that she has the capacity to do it if she chooses to do it—because she has already done it by focusing in this way in certain contexts. We can encourage her to do it and remind her to remind herself to do it. We can praise her when she actually does it, or tries to do it, or takes small steps forward.

We can also continue to remind her that she has the capacity to do almost anything she chooses to do in her life, if she chooses to do it and focuses fully on doing it.

## *Sharing connected focus experiences*

In pairs or small groups—partners, friends, classmates, teammates, families, workmates, or workshop participants share details about a specific experience where they felt totally focused or absolutely connected to something, someone, or some activity or experience. Give each person an opportunity to share one of his most fully connected focus experiences of his life. Ask him to describe his experience: "What were you doing, what did it feel like, what were you focused on / aware of, how do you think you were able to create or experience that fully focused connection during that experience or in that context?"

## Transferring fully connected focus experiences

In pairs or small groups, ask partners, friends, classmates, teammates, families, workmates, or participants to share ideas on how they feel they might be able to bring a more fully connected focus into different domains or experiences in their lives—such as at school, in conversations or meetings, relationships, sport practices, performances, or work. Give **everyone** an opportunity to share how he/she feels he/she can bring his/her best Game Focus or best-ever connected focus into everyday pursuits.

When we open ourselves to learning opportunities, opportunities open to us. When we fail to open ourselves to learning opportunities and the good things within us and around us, we live our lives as if those options and good qualities did not exist.

## Stop and shift your focus

Stop reading or doing whatever you are doing for a moment. Take a little break. Stretch your arms over your head, and then to the side. Bring your hands down so they are touching the back of your neck—and massage your neck. Slowly rotate your head around in a circle. Now focus on looking at what is in front of you. Look closely at something that is right there in front of you or near you, on your desk or wall or table or in the space you are in. Reach out and touch it. Feel what it feels like. Slowly turn your head and Focus on looking at what is to your right . . . and then to your left. Turn around and focus on what is behind you. Good . . . now you can go back to your reading.

## Focusing through distractions

The following two stories are shortened versions of two scripts that I wrote for one of my Positive Living Skills CDs that I use with children, teens, and adults (see Resource section for CDs). Each story is different but both are related to focusing and refocusing. Participants are asked to listen to only one story, which is a challenging focusing exercise, because two different stories are being played on the CD (or are being read aloud) at exactly the same time. Before listeners begin this focusing exercise, they are reminded to listen closely to only one of the stories and not to the other one. When both stories are finished, listeners get together in small groups (usually four to six people, half of which will listen to each story) and collectively retell as many details of their story as possible. The goal of this activity is to practice focusing through distractions and to remember the lessons from each story, both of which provide specific ways for dealing with distractions.

### 1. Umbalakiki

I once lived in a little jungle village in a country called Papua New Guinea. The people lived in little huts made from trees and big palm leaves. They had no electricity or TVs or stoves or bathtubs. The weather was warm all the time and there were lots of fruit trees and gardens and birds and rivers and streams. The people were very nice and friendly and the children loved to play together outside. They laughed a lot and had lots of fun playing.

When the children finished playing games, all the children on both teams got together in a circle. One of the children gently touched every other child on the arm or the shoulder, one by one and said, "Umbalakiki, Umbalakiki," which means, "I take it from you, I take it from you." She then placed her hand on a nearby tree.

The reason she did this was to take away any unhappy feelings, worries, or anger that may have come up during the game. This was a good way of taking away bad feelings, just in case any of the children were feeling bad. They called it Treeing It. The village chief, who was 110 years old, told me that his people have been doing this for many, many years. He told me that treeing negative or unhappy thoughts helps people to continue to live happily with each other and within themselves.

YOU can use Tree It to feel happier too. If ever you are feeling worried or unhappy or angry about something—in a sport or game or at home or in school—walk over to a tree, or a wall, or a door, or a garbage can and tree it. As you touch the wall or door or tree, pretend or imagine that you are putting all your worries or bad feelings in that tree or wall or door or garbage can. Then smile and walk away, knowing that you have let your worries go. You have put your worries away and you are now free to be positive and happy.

Now let's play a little pretend game in your mind to practice Umbalakiki.

Think of a not-so-happy feeling you once had. Imagine that you are taking that worry or bad feeling and walk over to a tree or door or garbage can. Touch your hand on the tree or wall or garbage can and say to yourself, "Umbalakiki—I am putting all those worries or bad feelings in here." Then smile and say to yourself, "Good—all those worries or bad feelings are now in the tree [or wall or garbage can]. I am now free to do something good and be happy." Imagine yourself doing something you like to do and feeling happy. Umbalakiki.

## 2. Changing Channels

In some ways you are like a TV or computer. You have lots of different channels inside you: happy channels and sad channels, grumpy and smiley, worried and relaxed, scary and fun, focused and not focused, angry and nice, good and bad, excited and calm, jumping up and down channels and sleepy channels. All of these channels are inside your head.

The great thing about being a person, and not a TV or computer, is that you can decide which channel you want to be on—every day. You have the power to choose which channel you are on today. You have the remote control switch inside you.

If you are on a channel that makes you grumpy and you don't want to be grumpy, or you feel better when you are not grumpy, you can change channels.

If you are on a worry channel and you don't want to worry right now, you can change channels.

If you are on a channel that makes you mad or angry, and you don't like being mad or don't want to be angry right now, you can change channels.

The way to change channels is to change what you are thinking about right now or change what you are doing right now. One way to do this is to press your thumb against your finger, as if you are changing channels with a remote control channel changer on your TV. Then think about something good, or happy, or calm, or relaxing, or fun, or funny that you have done or would like to do. You can change from a grumpy channel to a happy channel by remembering a Highlight or something special you really like to do.

When first learning to play Changing Channels, you might want to push the button on a real remote control TV channel changer and try to change channels in your own mind. Or you can play Changing Channels by imagining that the remote control switch is in your hand. To do this, you press your thumb against your finger as you change channels in your mind and make a click-click sound. You will get really good at changing channels by practicing changing channels. The best way to change channels is to pretend or imagine that the control switch is inside your head. Then you can change channels or shift focus any time you want just by thinking about the good channel you want to be on (click-click).

What channel do you want to be on today? Click on that channel right now and stay there for the rest of the day. When you are lying in bed, before you get up tomorrow morning, decide that you are going to be on a good mood channel, a nice channel, or a happy channel. If something makes you grumpy or not happy during the day, click back to a channel that makes you happier or more the way you like to be (click-click).

## *Focus on the positives*

One way to increase the frequency of connected focusing on positives and to decrease the times focused on negatives is to challenge children, adults, and yourself to focus only on positive things for specified periods of time. Set some goals to see if you and others can focus only on positive things, positive feelings, or positive actions (and absolutely nothing negative) for the next two minutes, five minutes, or ten minutes. Challenge your children to see if they can get up in the morning on a school day, get everything ready, share the bathroom, eat breakfast, and get to school, focusing only on the positives in themselves, others, and their day—nothing negative. Focus on the positives when you first get up in the morning; when you see your family members or friends; when you try something new; when playing games, going to practice, and arriving at work or school. Gradually increase the length of time you can focus on the positives.

## *Focus on being positive with others*

Children's overall positive focus is directly influenced by the extent to which they are treated in positive ways by parents, teachers, counselors, coaches, and other children. This activity is designed to enhance children's overall positive feelings experienced in school, at camp, in sport or other activities, and among family members at home. Children are asked to respond to the following two questions (with reference to other children, family members, teammates, teachers, coaches, or parents):

1. What are some things that other people (kids, teammates, teachers, coaches, parents) say or do that make you feel good?

2. What are some things they say or do that make you feel sad, mad, or bad?

Good things other children do might include: ask me to play with them, play with me, be nice to me, say something positive to me. Sad or bad things might include: leave me out, call me names, laugh at me, fight, tell me I'm no good, say I can't play.

List the things that make the children feel good on a large piece of paper and post it on the wall. Discuss the "feel good" things with the children and explain to them that if everyone does more of those feel-good things and less of the feel-bad things, everyone will feel better and have more fun. Set a group goal for everyone to treat each other in positive and respectful ways. Encourage children to tell other people how good it makes them feel when those people do or say something positive (e.g., "Thanks, that makes me feel really good"). Also encourage them to tell other people how it makes them feel when they do or say something negative (e.g., "That really wasn't very nice on my feelings; it made me feel bad. It would be a lot better and people would like you a lot more if you did or said something positive").

### *Share positive focus reminders*

In this activity, the participants clearly print, draw, color, type, or write down a few of their best Focus Reminders. One focus reminder is printed on each card (about the size of a 3 x 5-inch index card) or on a piece of paper. Their Focus Reminders might be something that you taught them (Be Here, Free Here, Focus, Connect, Be Positive), a reminder that they came up with on their own, or anything that they feel will help to remind them to focus—for example, a picture of a person, animal, or performer who is really focused. Each person shares one or two of their favorite Focus Reminders by holding up her or his piece of paper for others to see and saying the Reminder out loud for the group to hear. Participants are asked to Focus on Seeing, Hearing, and Remembering as many Focus Reminders as they can. They can also write down the Focus Reminders they liked best.

## Focus on Why You Can

The chances of learning more, performing well, or becoming a more positive person are greatly enhanced when participants focus on *why* they can do something or accomplish a goal. Before participants try to do something, learn something, or attempt new skills, ask them to focus on why they can do this or accomplish this goal. Focusing on Why You

Can frees people of all ages to focus on the positives and greatly increases their chances of doing what they want and prefer to do.

## My Personal Experiences with Fully Focused Connections

When I feel most fully connected in my life experiences, I feel a pure, effortless connection. I am simply "being fully here" in the moment, in this second, and nowhere else. For me there is also a sense of not "trying." I know that I want to be fully in the moment and let that happen or free it to happen. I am usually most connected when my mind is clear . . . there are no other thoughts . . . I am just feeling what I am feeling . . . and doing what I am doing. This happens often, every day, in the activities I do; for example, when I am writing or playing or running or walking or paddling in nature. It also happens in conversations or consulting sessions, where I am totally connected and everything else disappears. I feel like my feelings are completely connected with the person who is sharing her or his feelings. There is no feeling of separation. I am feeling beyond the words—really feeling what that person is feeling. When my focus is fully connected, it is not just words or movements or objects, going back and forth, it is connected feelings flowing freely between two beings—or one being and what he or she is engaged in.

When I am most fully connected, I feel like I *become* the experience. I lose myself in the experience and at the same time enrich myself by finding a better part of myself from being so absorbed within the experience. During my most connected moments, I am not making any value judgments or evaluating anyone, anything, or any movement or experience—I am just totally connecting with the opportunity, the person, or the experience. I become the experience. That's what a fully connected focus feels like for me and brings to me—every day.

## Free Practice

One of the great things about a Connected Focus is that you can practice doing it in everything you do or try to do—every day of your life. And there is no user fee for doing it, no matter where you are or what you are doing! You can practice your fully Connected Focus when you are reading books or e-mails, playing games, listening to music, speaking with someone, or listening when someone is speaking to you. There are a million ways you can connect your focus. If you take advantage of even a few of those ways every day, you will give yourself one of the greatest gifts of life: a fully connected focus!

## My Experiences with High-level Performers' Fully Focused Connections

The greatest athletes and other high-level performers with whom I have worked over many years perform their best when they give themselves to their performance, lose themselves within it, and become inseparable from what they are doing. They free themselves to connect totally with their performance. Nothing else in the world exists for them during those connected moments in time. In their best and most flowing performances, there is an element of freedom and trust—in their preparation, body, focus, and intuition—that leads them without conscious thought. These performers already have great physical and technical skills. They simply need to free their focus from other things so they can connect fully, and remain completely connected, with what they are doing for the duration of their performance (see *In Pursuit of Excellence* in the Resource section).

## Five Steps to Strengthen Your Focus

1.  **Choose to Connect** fully with listening, seeing, learning, playing, performing, reading, feeling, loving, enjoying, and reflecting, and live the focusing lessons learned.

2.  **Choose to Practice** connecting your focus in different activities, games, interactions, learning, training, and performance contexts.

3.  **Choose to Extend** the time your focus is fully connected in different parts of your life.

4.  **Choose to Focus** on the positives in yourself, your day, your experiences, and your life.

5.  **Continue to Nurture** and refine your connected stream of focus so you live more, learn more, perform better, remember more, see more, feel more, and find more joy in each experience and each day.

## Evaluate the Depth of Your Focus

Rate the depth of your focus in activities or pursuits that are important to you. You can do this in writing or on a rating scale from 0 to 10: A zero being not focused at all, a 10 being absolutely totally connected, and a 5 being somewhere in between.

## Evaluate the Length of Your Focus

Reflect on the duration of your focus in activities or pursuits that are important to you. You can do this by writing down how long you feel you were connected, when you were most connected, and when you lost your connection. In some contexts you can also use a stopwatch to clock the duration of your focus. For example, how long you are remaining focused in different contexts of your life: "listening" in a class, being fully engaged in training, practices, performances, reading, doing assignments, working, working out, talking on the phone, interacting with people you care about or don't care about, or doing whatever is important to you or of value to others. You don't have to clock your focus every time you do something, but it is valuable to do it in pursuits or interactions that are important to you—at least once every week or two. Reflecting on the depth and duration of your focus gives you a good idea of where you are with your focus and how you are progressing. It is also a great reminder to continue to stay focused, especially in things that are important to you and to others in your life.

## Embrace the Magic Moments (M&M's)

A positive, fully connected focus makes the difference between a connected and a disconnected experience, conversation, learning experience, or performance; an opportunity embraced and an opportunity missed; a connected life and a disconnected life; a Highlight and a No-light. A No-light is when you just do not see the light because you are not focused.

Life's magic moments inspire us and give us positive, life-enhancing energy—even when they are simple little things. Magic moments are made possible through a positive, fully connected focus. These are the moments when you free yourself—and sometimes the situation or experience helps free you—from all other thoughts, issues, and concerns. Your focus connects fully and absolutely with the experience in which you are engaged, and nothing else. You free yourself to connect, and the depth of the connection makes the moment special or magical. Magic moments do not have to be limited to a few experiences in your life. They can become a normal part of everyday living when you learn to sustain your focus in positive and flowing ways. Practice connecting with simple everyday opportunities: in nature, physical activity, personal discoveries, and with good friends and positive people who open themselves to positive, life-enhancing connections that go beyond the surface.

Magic moments come from creating a deeper level of connection, from becoming inseparable from the special moments you are experiencing. They cannot be experienced by skimming through life on the surface, or going through the motions of doing something, or being with someone or something in a distant or disconnected way. We all have the capacity to open ourselves to pure connections, not only in the biggest events of life but also within the simplest moments. "Ordinary" moments become "extraordinary" when we open ourselves to experience and live those moments on a deeper level.

## Lessons Learned from Focusing Activities

1. There are many things within us and around us that we never fully connect with, look at, see, feel, hear, focus on, or learn from.

2. We can connect and improve our focusing skills by choosing to bring our fully connected focus with us every day.

3. When we take a few minutes to really connect with something or someone, we begin to see, feel, and understand that almost every experience or person is unique and of value in some way.

4. We can learn and gain from almost any situation when we bring a fully connected focus into that context or interaction—even when at first glance it may appear to be uninteresting or not worthy of our connection.

5. There are many good reasons to continue to focus in positive and fully connected ways with people, activities, learning and performance opportunities, animals, flowers, trees, oceans, streams, and thousands of other things.

## How Important Are Focusing Skills?

Focusing skills are the most important human skills for enhancing positive learning, positive performance, and positive living. A fully connected focus can open many doors to living more positive, productive, and meaningful lives. Teaching focusing skills on a global level will give everyone an opportunity to get the best out of themselves and contribute their best to others.

## Teaching and Coaching Focus

Teaching focusing skills is essential for helping all people continue to learn, perform, and grow in positive ways. This can begin right now by teaching school-aged children and youth to focus in more positive and fully connected ways in school, at home, and in every learning, performance, and life context. With teens, adults, athletes, and other performers, I often start by asking them to respond to the following questions (in writing) or begin with a discussion about their experiences with Focus.

1.  What does Focus or being focused mean to you?

2.  What is a Fully Connected Focus for you? What do you feel when you are most fully connected in a performance or in some other part of your life?

3.  Share a specific example of a time when you felt your focus was fully connected—a time when you were totally absorbed with what you were doing, feeling, seeing, hearing, or experiencing—and for that period of time were not aware of anything else.

4.  What is the difference between your best focus and your less-than-best or worst focus?

5.  Do you think a Fully Connected Focus is important for you? If yes, why? How can it help you? How can it help other people? (If no, why do you think it is not important?)

6.  What do you think you can do to improve your focus so it is more fully connected (or at its best) for longer periods of time in different parts of your day and different parts of your life?

## *Can everyone learn focusing skills?*

Focusing is a teachable and sustainable skill that virtually everyone can learn and improve. When young children are playing, most of them are fully engaged in their play. Nothing distracts them or gets in the way of their connection with their play, so we know they are capable of focusing. Almost everyone is capable of developing a purely connected focus in something they do. We can help children, teens, or adults to focus better by engaging them in Focusing Activities and by asking them to remember the times in their life when they were most fully connected. We can then encourage them and challenge them to focus or connect in this fully connected way more often in different contexts. We can continue encouraging them to focus in connected ways. See if you can really listen to me when I am talking to you. See if you can remember what you read in this paragraph. See if you can really *be here* when you are doing this activity or assignment. See if you can let everything else go and just focus on doing this move, task, or assignment. See if you can connect fully with what you are doing and make the best of this opportunity.

*See if you can focus on taking this step—even if it is only for a few seconds. Just focus on doing what you are doing right now.*

Follow up with participants by asking them if they tried to focus, and if they did try, ask them how it went. Ask them how they think they can make it better or stay focused longer next time. If they didn't try to focus or were not able to do it, set another focusing goal and ask them to try again. Continue to play some of the simplest focusing activities in this chapter when you are with them. This will help them to make progress, and once they start rolling forward, they usually keep rolling in a positive direction.

Most people are already able to create a fully focused connection with something in their lives, at least for short periods of time. If they know they can do it sometimes, they probably know that they are capable of connecting that way more often. As people gain a clearer understanding of how they can enter that fully focused connection and what it feels like, they put themselves in a better position to experience it more often. The ultimate focusing goal is to make that focused connection as pure as it can be and to sustain that connection for progressively longer periods of time in different contexts.

## Improving Your Focusing Skills

Focusing is a skill that can be learned, practiced, and improved or perfected—like any other skill. The more you practice connecting, the easier it is to reach a fully connected state. The better you understand your best focus and what that focus feels like, the easier it is to free it to happen. In the end, focusing is a freedom experience—as opposed to something that feels forced.

What frees your own best-focused connection? Does it happen when you are interacting with other people, or when you are trying to learn something, or when you are working, performing, dancing, or doing something you love to do? The better you understand what frees you to connect fully, the better the chances of freeing that fully focused connection more often.

When I work as a focus coach with athletes and high-level performers in other domains, I often remind them to "Just free yourself to connect with what you are doing" (and clear your mind of everything else). I do this because I know if they follow this simple advice they will almost always do what they are capable of doing. Best performances are rarely, if ever, forced. When you try to force a performance or to force a connection with a person, you usually lose the connection. Best performances and best connections usually come with a freeing-up feeling. When you simply free yourself to be fully there and embrace each moment of the experience, the connected focus usually leads you in positive ways and remains with you.

## *Distractions*

Sometimes distractions do come in and momentarily break the connection—for people at all levels, in all disciplines, and in all circumstances. To prepare for this possibility, I work with people in two ways.

1. I help them to prevent distractions from coming in by being so focused and so fully connected with what they are doing that they don't even notice the potential distractions.

2. I help them to develop a refocusing plan to reconnect their focus quickly in case they are distracted. If you lose your focused connection, or your focus is not where you want it to be, you need a way to reconnect. One effective way to bring your focus back to where you would prefer it to be is to use a preplanned word, image, or focus reminder. It could be something as simple as "Be here." Focus Reminders are often tied in with your breathing. You breathe in and out slowly and remind yourself to "Be here." Or you focus on breathing easily and slowly and remind yourself to reconnect; or remember a confident, connected feeling that you had in the past that you would like to bring into this experience or performance. Purely focused connections come from connecting fully with a feeling you want to feel that frees you to do what you want to do.

We can empower all people to live more productive, meaningful, and joyful lives by teaching them positive and fully connected focusing skills, regardless of the circumstances in which they are currently living.

# 11

# RELAXATION AND JOYFUL LIVING

### *Every day is Relaxation Day.*

**R**elaxation enhances focusing, learning, and performance and adds balance, joy, and quality to life. Everyone benefits from moments of pure relaxation—every day.

Ever feel like you are running on a treadmill or spinning your wheels all day long? Too many things to do . . . too little time to do them: studying, preparing, training, working; away too much or not enough; making meals, cleaning, shopping, washing; shuttling children, family members, or others to multiple activities. Worrying too much and relaxing too little? Do YOU set aside times for yourself to relax fully, regenerate completely, and live joyfully? Every day? If you do, great! If you don't, now is the time to begin!

One of the best ways to teach people who are close to your heart the value of relaxation, balance, and joyful living is to provide a positive example yourself. Another best way is to teach them relaxation skills. You can begin this process with some of the relaxation activities presented in this chapter. Collectively, we can all benefit from teaching children, youth, adults, and ourselves to relax more fully and embrace a healthier lifestyle.

People whose lives are out of balance or who live with too much stress and too little relaxation definitely put their lives at risk and sometimes turn to medications, prescription drugs, illegal drugs, or alcohol, to escape, relax, or sleep; or in an attempt to fill the void for what they are missing in their lives. This path destroys the quality of many lives. Everyone is capable of learning to relax themselves on their own so they can sleep well, reduce the stress in their lives, and find joy in relaxation and a sense of meaning in their lives. The earlier we begin to teach people how to do this, the better for everyone.

A life that includes daily relaxation or moments of silence—to simply relax, reflect, and regenerate mentally, physically, and emotionally—is the best path to positive, balanced living. Meaningful work that leads to worthy contributions to others is a definite advantage. However, *more* work is not necessarily *better* work. Less volume with higher quality, combined with creating time-outs for relaxation, reflection, and recovery is often the best and most sustainable path to positive living, positive performance, and making the most meaningful contributions.

For people with busy lives, demanding careers, growing families, or multiple demands, nothing is more important than embracing pure moments of joyful relaxation every day.

## Why Is Relaxation Important?

Relaxation helps people of all ages in the following ways:

1. **Stress reduction.** Relaxation helps us to prevent unnecessary stress, lower the intensity of stress, and shorten the duration of stress.

2. **Recovery from stress.** Relaxation helps us to recover more quickly from fatigue and reduces the potential harmful effects of stress.

3. **More restful sleep.** Relaxation helps us to go to sleep more quickly and easily, experience a longer and more restful sleep, and go back to sleep more quickly if we wake up.

4. **Better focus.** Relaxation helps us to connect our focus more effectively and easily for learning, performances, and personal interactions—especially in stressful situations.

5. **Stronger immune system.** Relaxation helps us to stay strong and healthy longer. An ongoing diet of stress weakens our immune system and opens the door to many different kinds of illnesses. Relaxing more often helps us to become and remain stronger, healthier, and more balanced.

6. **Enhanced quality of life.** Relaxation helps us to embrace peaceful moments of silence and experience simple daily joys that lift the quality of every day and the joyfulness of every life.

7. **Relaxation adds years to our lives and life to our years.**

# Teaching Children, Youth, and Adults to Relax

Anyone, at any age, can learn to relax and improve his/her skills for relaxing, in virtually any context. You can begin teaching children to relax in preschool or kindergarten by leading them in some of the relaxation activities in this chapter. Children enjoy listening to the relaxation activities on the Positive Living Skills CDs (especially "Spaghetti Toes" and "Jelly Belly"). Set aside specific times every day for your children, teenagers, family members, students, athletes, and performers, as well as yourself, to simply relax, regenerate, re-energize, embrace moments of silence, or connect fully with a simple, positive, relaxation experience. Do it because your children, students, and others are worth it, and your life is worth it. You will be helping yourself and others to live with more joy and quality. When people are relaxed and focused, they can learn more, perform better, and feel happier within themselves and their relationships.

## Learning to Relax and Focus with Positive Living Skills CDs

The simplest way to begin to teach groups, classes, or individuals to relax is to use the CDs I designed specifically for this purpose. The *Positive Living Skills Series* CDs 1–4 were created specifically to teach children, youth, and others to relax and focus in positive ways. We have used these CD activities in all our child- and youth-based intervention programs. They have proven to be very effective for teaching children and people of all ages to relax and learn a variety of Positive Living Skills within a short period of time.

All of the Positive Living Skills CDs (including those designed to enhance focusing and refocusing skills) begin by asking participants to focus on their breathing: *Breathe in slowly . . . Breathe out slowly . . . Let yourself relax.* I do this for two good reasons. First, when listeners relax by focusing on their breathing—before they begin listening to a CD story or activity—it helps them to remove outside distractions and gets them focused on listening to the CD exercise. Second, participants get lots of practice relaxing within the space of a few relaxing breaths because every CD activity begins by asking them to relax and focus on their breathing.

Many children and youth have used Positive Living Skills CDs to relax, focus, and refocus—for example, while going to sleep at night, when getting needles from a nurse or doctor, going to the dentist, giving speeches in front of classes, or speaking to large audiences; or when singing, dancing, acting, or performing in sport or other situations where they are being judged or evaluated. These same CD relaxation and refocusing activities have been very helpful for hospitalized children who are experiencing high levels of stress or facing life-threatening illness (as well as their parents) and for children with attention deficits and/or hyperactivity disorders.

I also have a second CD series (*Zone of Excellence Series* CDs 1–4), which has been used by high-performance athletes and performers in other domains to help them relax, sleep more soundly before and after big events, and prepare themselves to focus and refocus on the right things during training, practices, and performances. (See the Resource section for more information on all CDs.)

## What Is Relaxation?

Elementary school children in our Positive Living Skills Program were asked: "What is relaxation?" Here are a few of their responses.

- Relaxation is like stretching out in the sun, feeling warm and relaxed and happy. (Seven-year-old)

- Relaxation is when you lie down and breathe slowly. Your troubles disappear. You just feel calm and good — like you're free. (Nine-year-old)

- Relaxation is when you let your whole body go loose and forget your worries. (Ten-year-old)

- Stress is like when you pull a rubber band all the way to the end and it's about to snap. Relaxation is when you let the rubber band go loose and free. (Eleven-year-old)

Relaxation for five- and six-year-olds is . . .

- When you're like cooked spaghetti

- When nothing bugs you

- When you are feeling nice and cozy

- Letting out all the worries

- Like floating on a cloud

# Teaching People of All Ages to Relax

Everyone can learn to relax. In our Positive Living Skills educational and intervention programs, we begin with some of the following relaxation activities, which can be done almost anytime and anywhere: in a classroom, gym, park, living room, office, hospital, practice area, or performance setting; while traveling or before going to sleep at night. Relaxation activities can be done effectively with large groups of people, small teams, classes, in pairs, or with one child, teenager, or adult doing the relaxation exercise alone.

When presenting relaxation activities to groups of children or youth in their classrooms, participants usually sit at their desks and relax with their heads resting on the desk. In classrooms that have enough space, or gymnasiums, at summer camps, or in training settings, participants usually lie down and relax on the floor or on the ground. In homes, apartments, hospitals, or treatment centers, participants usually lie down and relax on a bed, sofa, mat, rug, floor, or the grass in an outdoor setting.

When first beginning relaxation exercises, it is helpful to turn off anything that is making noise, dim the lights, and ask participants to close their eyes. This helps to eliminate some potential external distractions—such as other people or electronic devices. Try to create an environment that gives participants the best chance of closing off outside distractions so they can focus only on relaxing and the positive feelings associated with the relaxation activity. As participants get better at relaxing, external distractions can be allowed or even introduced, and participants can be challenged to continue to focus only on relaxing or on what they are doing, no matter what is going on around them. Simulating real-world conditions where participants want to relax and focus only on what they are doing in the face of distractions is a good thing. However, intentional distractions should be introduced only after participants have learned, practiced, and perfected some basic strategies for relaxation and refocusing.

# Starting the Relaxation Training Process

Before beginning each relaxation activity, ask the participants to sit or lie down in a comfortable position. If they are lying down, ask them to stretch their legs straight out in front of them and rest their arms quietly at their sides. Ensure that there is enough space between participants so that they are not being touched or distracted by anyone else. If it is not feasible for participants to lie down, ask them to sit comfortably with their heads down, resting in a relaxed position at their desk or table.

When the participants are quiet, comfortable, and ready to begin the relaxation activity, start the CD relaxation activity you have selected or read one of the following relaxation scripts, stories, or focusing exercises to the participants. Ask them to focus only on listening to your voice or the voice on the CD for the next few minutes and focus on doing exactly what "the voice" is asking them to do.

Remind participants that the best way to tune out unwanted or disruptive distractions is to focus completely on listening to the voice and doing what the voice is asking them to do—and nothing else. Encourage participants to focus fully on relaxing and listening to the CD (or your voice) so that all external or internal distractions disappear naturally.

## *Spaghetti Toes*

Spaghetti Toes is a great relaxation activity to begin with, especially for young children. This activity is designed to give children practice at "focusing into" different parts of their body. Spaghetti Toes draws upon the image of cooked spaghetti to help children create and send relaxing messages to various muscles in their bodies. The first time you introduce this activity, if possible, start by giving each child a piece of **uncooked spaghetti**. Let the children examine it closely to see and feel how stiff it is, and how easily it breaks. Then give each child a piece of **cooked spaghetti** (warm, if possible). Let them examine it to see and feel how flexible it is and how easily it can curl up or wiggle without breaking.

Point out that stiff, hard, tense, uncooked spaghetti breaks or snaps more easily than soft, relaxed, flexible, cooked spaghetti. People are a bit like that, too.

Once they are ready to begin the Spaghetti Toes activity, remind the participants to listen closely; then start the CD track ("Spaghetti Toes") or read the following script to the participants. With preschool children, you may want to shorten the script. Most of the scripts presented in this book (and many more) are available on my *Positive Living Skills* CDs (see Resource section).

Get yourself into a comfortable position. Close your eyes and just listen to my voice. Breathe in slowly. Breathe out slowly. Breathe in slowly. Breathe out slowly. Let yourself relax. Continue to breathe in slowly and breathe out slowly—and just listen to my voice—while I tell you a story about Spaghetti Toes.

I wonder how good you are at talking to your toes. I'll bet you are pretty good. Let's find out.

Tell the toes on one of your feet to wiggle. Are they wiggling? On just one foot? Good! Now tell these toes to stop wiggling. Tell the toes on your other foot to wiggle. Tell them to wiggle real slow . . . and faster . . . and real slow again . . . slower . . . stop. Did your toes listen to you? Good.

If you talk to different parts of your body, like you just did with your toes, your body will listen to you . . . especially if you talk to it a lot. I'm going to show you how you can be the boss of your mind and body by talking to it.

First I want to tell you something about spaghetti. I like spaghetti. I'll bet you do, too. Did you ever see spaghetti before it's cooked? It's kind of cold and hard and stiff and it's easy to break. When it's cooked, it's warm and soft and it kinda lies down and curls up on your plate.

I want to see if you can talk to your toes to get them to go soft and warm and sleepy like spaghetti lying on your plate. You might have to talk to them quite a bit to make them know what you want them to do, but I know they can do it.

Wiggle your toes on one foot. Now tell those toes to stop wiggling. Tell them to go soft and sleepy like warm spaghetti lying on your plate. Now wiggle the toes on your other foot. Stop wiggling. Turn those toes into soft spaghetti. Good.

Wiggle one leg. Stop wiggling. Now tell that leg to go soft and sleepy like warm spaghetti. Now wiggle the other leg. Stop. Tell it to go soft and sleepy. Wiggle your bum (behind or backside). Let it go soft and sleepy.

Wiggle your fingers on one hand. Tell your fingers to stop wiggling. See if you can make those fingers feel warm and soft and sleepy like spaghetti lying on your plate. Now wiggle your fingers on your other hand. Slowly. Stop. Make those fingers feel warm. Tell them to go soft and sleepy.

Now wiggle one arm. Stop. Tell your arm to go soft and sleepy. Now wiggle the other arm. Tell it to go soft and sleepy. Good.

Let your whole *you* go soft and warm and sleepy like soft spaghetti lying on your plate. [Pause.] That's really good. Your body is listening well. [Pause.] Let your body stay like warm spaghetti and just listen to me. I want to tell you about when spaghetti toes can help you.

When you are worried or scared, or when something hurts, your toes and your hands and muscles get kinda hard and stiff—like hard spaghetti before it's cooked. If you are worried or scared or something hurts, you feel a lot better and it doesn't hurt so much if your hands and toes and muscles are like warm, soft spaghetti lying on a plate. If you practice doing your spaghetti toes you'll get real good at it. Then you can tell your hands and toes and muscles to help you by going warm and soft and sleepy, even if you are worried or something hurts.

Before you go, let's try talking to your mouth. Wiggle your mouth. Let it go soft and sleepy. Wiggle your tongue. Let it go soft and sleepy. Wiggle your eyebrows. Let them go soft and sleepy. Let your whole *you* go warm and soft and sleepy. Let your whole *you* feel good.

At the end of the "Spaghetti Toes" activity (and other relaxation activities), ask the children or participants to gradually sit up or stand up and stretch their arms over their heads. Then ask them to sit down and share their thoughts about what it felt like to do "Spaghetti Toes" and where they think they might be able to use it in the future.

## *Jelly Belly*

Jelly Belly is another great relaxation activity to begin with, especially for young children. Older children and teenagers also like Jelly Belly but will probably be more keen to try it in a group if you tell them that athletes and other high-level performers use this kind of relaxation. Or tell them this activity is for little kids but you thought they might be interested in hearing what the little kids are doing for their relaxation.

This activity is designed to help children learn how to do diaphragmatic breathing (breathing with the abdomen or stomach). This can relax the body quickly (within a few breaths) and is a more efficient way of breathing than the normal chest breathing. When you extend your diaphragm muscle as you breathe in, you take in about 20 percent more air because you are able to fill the lower lung with air. Many classical singers, musicians, and high-performance athletes are taught diaphragmatic breathing because of its immediate relaxation effect and its performance advantages.

The first time you introduce this activity, if possible start by making some Jell-O, together with the participants, using a mold or a little bowl (or bring in some Jell-O that is already made). Once it is set, let the participant wiggle it and jiggle it. Then tell them they can eat it after doing Jelly Belly.

Once you are ready to begin the Jelly Belly activity, remind the participants to listen closely, then start the CD track ("Jelly Belly") or read the following script to the participants.

Get yourself into a comfortable position. Close your eyes and just listen to my voice.

Breathe in slowly. Breathe out slowly. Breathe in slowly. Breathe out slowly. Let yourself relax. Continue to breathe in slowly and breathe out slowly, and just listen to my voice while I tell you a story about Jelly Belly.

There are lots of focus games you can play with your mind and body. This one is called "Jelly Belly." I wonder how good you are at talking to your belly. I'll bet you are pretty good. Let's find out.

Have you ever heard of Jell-O? Well, this game is called Jelly Belly. It is a game you play by breathing into your own body and it's kind of like filling a bowl with jelly. It's a little tricky, but I think you can do it.

Put one of your hands right on top of your belly button. See if you can breathe in air slowly and gently, until your belly pushes your hand up. Now see if you can breathe out slowly so that your hand sinks down on your belly. Breathe in—let your belly push your hand up slowly. Breathe out—let your hand sink down gently. As you breathe in, feel your belly slowly fill right up to your belly button. Feel your belly gently push your hand way up.

As you breathe out, let your belly sink way down until it feels empty. Feel your belly slowly pull your hand way down.

Breathe in—belly way up
Breathe out—belly way down
Breathe in—belly way up
Breathe out—belly way down
Breathe in—belly way up
Breathe out—belly way down
[Repeat the in-and-out phase five times]

Good! Now I'd like you to just breathe easily and slowly. Each time you breathe out, say to yourself, "Relax." Let your whole *you* go soft and warm and sleepy. [Pause twenty seconds.] Good.

You feel really relaxed. You feel really good. Your body feels really good. You made your body feel good by talking to it. The more you talk to your body, the more it listens to you and the more it does what you want it to do. You are the boss of your belly and your body.

At the end of the Jelly Belly activity (and other relaxation activities), ask the children or participants to gradually sit up or stand up and stretch their arms over their heads. Then ask them to sit down and to share their thoughts about what it felt like to do Jelly Belly—and when they think they might be able to use Jelly Belly.

## Jelly Belly on the Move

Once children/participants have done Jelly Belly (diaphragmatic breathing) a couple of times with the CD or Jelly Belly script, encourage them to practice doing Jelly Belly on their own in different contexts. For example, ask them to try Jelly Belly breathing when they are standing, walking, talking, singing, running, reading, playing games or sports, sitting at their desks, or sharing something in front of a group.

## Floating on Clouds

Floating on Clouds is a simple relaxation activity for young children. They imagine or pretend that they are floating on top of a big fluffy cloud in the sky. Introduce this activity by talking to the children about clouds, looking at clouds in the sky, or showing them pictures of big fluffy clouds.

When they are ready to begin the Floating on Clouds activity, remind them to listen closely, then start the CD track ("Floating on Clouds") or read the following script to the children.

> Lie down or sit down. Get yourself into a comfortable position. Gently close your eyes and just listen to my voice. Breathe in slowly. Breathe out slowly. Breathe in slowly. Breathe out slowly. Let yourself relax. Continue to breathe in slowly and breathe out slowly and just listen to my voice while we try Floating on Clouds.
>
> There are lots of focus games you can play with your mind and body. This one is called "Floating on Clouds." I

wonder how good you are at Floating on Clouds. I'll bet you are pretty good. Let's find out.

Imagine that you are outside in a beautiful, quiet place. It is a lovely day. Everything feels warm and happy. Everything around you is completely quiet. You are lying down looking up at the clouds—big, white, soft, fluffy clouds—in the beautiful blue sky. As you breathe in, you begin to float gently off the ground. You float up and up slowly and gently, to a big fluffy cloud in the sky. You float right up over top of the cloud and gently sink into the cloud. You are now floating on top of a big fluffy white cloud. Your arms and legs are stretched out wide and you are floating on the biggest, softest cloud that is floating in the sky.

You feel so good, and so relaxed, and so calm, floating on your cloud. It makes you feel good all over. You are strong. You are happy. You are healthy. You feel as if you can do anything. You feel good energy from your cloud. Good feelings spread through your entire body and mind as you float gently, enjoying your ride on your special cloud.

Whenever you want to float back down to the earth, just tell your cloud, and it will float you gently down, down, down to the ground. Once you are safely stretched out on the ground, your cloud floats back up to its home in the sky. It smiles at you. You smile at it. Floating on your cloud is fun. Any time you want to really relax, or any time you are worried about something, you can go for a float on your cloud. Your cloud is always happy to have you visit.

## *Relaxed breathing*

Get yourself into a comfortable position. Close your eyes and just listen to my voice. Breathe in slowly. Breathe out slowly. Breathe in slowly. Breathe out slowly. Let yourself relax. For the next three breaths, as you breathe in, feel your body filling with air and as you breathe out, say to yourself, "Relax . . . relax . . . relax." Feel the relaxation spread through your body. [Pause.] Good.

Now listen closely to the sound of your own breathing. As you breathe in, listen to the sound of the air going into your body. As you breathe out, listen to the sound of the air leaving your body. [Pause for a few breaths.] Good.

Now focus on the feeling of your own breathing. As you breathe in, feel the air going into your body. As you breathe out, feel the air leaving your body. [Pause.] Good.

You are feeling good. You are feeling relaxed. You are in control. Whenever you are tense, or want to relax, follow your breathing. Breathe easily and slowly. This will free you to relax, listen, and enjoy whatever you are doing.

Continue to breathe easily and slowly. Feel yourself relax. As you breathe out, say to yourself, "Relax . . . relax . . . relax." Let your whole body relax.

Good. You are sinking into a calm and wonderful state of complete relaxation.

For the next few breaths, continue to follow your breathing. Breathe easily and slowly. As you breathe in, allow your stomach to rise and extend. As you breathe out, let your whole body relax. Breathe in—feel your stomach rise. Breathe out—relax. Breathe in—feel your stomach rise. Breathe out—relax. For the next five breaths, each time you breathe in, feel your stomach rise—each time you breathe out, say to yourself, "Relax." [Pause five breaths.]

Good. You are calm. You are relaxed. You feel confident and happy to be alive. You are in control of your mind and body. You feel great.

Whenever you want to relax, take in one long, slow breath, and as you breathe out, think to yourself, "Relax." This will put you back in control.

You've done a great job relaxing yourself. Now slowly stretch your arms to the side, or over your head—then open your eyes and have a great day.

## *Flowing Stream*

Flowing stream is an excellent way to help children, teens, and adults learn to flow through various challenges and obstacles and take advantage of the many opportunities they have in their day and in their lives. Flowing like a stream is a way of seeing life and different events in your life as opportunities that you can flow through in positive ways every day.

If you are fortunate enough to live near a flowing stream, go out and look at that flowing stream and take others to look at it with you. Let them watch, hear, feel, and really "see" the water flowing. If there are no real streams nearby, consider going out on a field trip into nature, where you and others can really look closely at a flowing stream. If real flowing streams are not a possibility, find some DVD clips of water flowing down a stream, where you can see and hear the water gently flowing. Participants can look at these flowing images and carry them into the following "Flowing Stream" activity.

When participants are ready to begin the Flowing Stream activity, remind them to listen closely, then start the CD track ("Flowing Stream") or read the following script to the participants.

> Get yourself into a comfortable position. Close your eyes and just listen to my voice.
>
> Breathe in slowly. Breathe out slowly. Breathe in slowly. Breathe out slowly. Let yourself relax. Continue to breathe in slowly and breathe out slowly and just listen to my voice while I tell you a story about Flowing Streams.
>
> There are lots of focus games you can play with your mind and body. This one is called "Flowing Stream." I wonder how good you are at Flowing like a Stream. I'll bet you are pretty good. Let's find out.
>
> Imagine that you are outside, sitting or lying quietly next to a beautiful little stream. The sun is shining, the sky is blue, the air is fresh. The rays of sunshine are sparkling off the surface of the crystal-clear water as it flows gently along. You can feel the warmth of the sun reflecting on your face and hear the sounds of the water flow-

ing. You feel good. You feel calm. You feel happy to be alive.

Listen to the relaxing sounds of the water flowing gently down the stream.

Let those relaxed feelings flow gently through your own mind and body [pause].

Continue to relax while I tell you a story about flowing through obstacles like a stream.

If you watch water flowing down a river or stream, you will see that it always finds a path. It finds its own path, even if there are big obstacles like rocks, branches, or logs along the way. Without worry, it simply flows around, over, or through any obstacles along its path. It keeps flowing toward its destination.

You can flow around many obstacles, worries, or setbacks in your day and in your life, just like a stream. There are ways around, over, or through almost all obstacles—if you relax and let yourself flow. If ever you are stressed or discouraged or facing a big obstacle, imagine that you are like the water flowing gently along like a river or stream.

For a brief time, become that stream. Enter the flowing stream channel. See where it takes you. Let the relaxation flow through you and within you, like a crystal-clear stream flowing gently down a mountain.

Let the flow of the water carry you over, around, under, or through the obstacles or worries. Keep flowing toward your destination.

Continue to believe in yourself along the way.

Continue to believe in what you are doing.

Flow through the obstacles.

Follow your own best path.

Follow the best path for the people you love.

## Muscle relaxation

Get yourself into a comfortable position. Close your eyes and just listen to my voice. Breathe in slowly. Breathe out slowly. Breathe in slowly. Breathe out slowly. [Pause.] Let yourself relax. Feel the relaxation spread through your body. Good.

Now I'd like you to *think into* different body parts I mention and let those body parts relax. Let's start with your feet. Move your toes slightly. Let them relax. Now think into your lower legs. Let the muscles in your lower legs totally relax. Think into your upper legs. Let those muscles totally relax. Feel your legs sink into a completely relaxed state. Relax your behind. [Pause.]

Focus on the muscles in your lower back. Think relaxation into those muscles. Feel the relaxation spread into your upper back. Feel your whole body sink into a deep state of relaxation. Now focus on your fingers. Feel them tingle slightly. Think warmth into your fingers. Let them totally relax. Relax your lower arms, your upper arms, and your shoulders. Totally relax. Relax your neck. [Pause.] And your jaw. Feel your head sink into a totally relaxed and comfortable position.

Scan your body for possible areas of tightness and relax those areas. Feel your entire body encircled with soothing warmth and relaxation. Enjoy this wonderful state of complete relaxation. [Pause about one minute.]

Good. You are calm. You are relaxed. You feel confident and happy to be alive. You are in control of yourself and your body. You feel great.

You've done a great job relaxing yourself. Now slowly stretch your arms to the side, open your eyes, and have a great day.

## *Special place relaxation*

Get yourself into a comfortable position. Close your eyes and listen to my voice. Breathe in slowly. Breathe out slowly. Breathe in slowly. Breathe out slowly. [Pause.] Let yourself relax. Feel the relaxation spread through your body.

Each time you breathe out, feel yourself sink deeper and deeper into a calm and wonderful state of complete relaxation. [Pause.]

Now in your imagination I'd like you to go to a very special place. This is your own special place. It is the most beautiful and most relaxing place you can imagine. You can go here whenever you want to feel calm, peaceful, and relaxed.

In your special place it is warm; it is quiet; it is beautiful. You are totally relaxed, enjoying the warmth and calmness of your special place. [Pause thirty seconds.] Feel the warmth. Feel the stillness. Enjoy the silence. Enjoy the beauty.

In your special place it is so relaxing. You are calm. You are relaxed. You feel confident and happy to be alive. You are in control of yourself and the things you do. You feel great.

Feel the calmness spread through your entire body and mind as you rest gently, enjoying the peace, tranquility, and special feeling of your special place. You feel so good, and so relaxed. You are comfortable; you are warm; you are safe. You are in control of your focus, mind, and body. Enjoy this wonderful, restful state. Whenever you are tense, remember the feeling of your special place. Go there to find peace and relaxation.

## *Standing relaxation*

Once children, youth, or adults are capable of relaxing in a stretched-out position on a mat, on the floor, in their own homes in bed, or relaxing while sitting at their desks, ask them to try relaxing while they are standing.

Stand up. Stretch your arms slowly over your head. Lower your arms and let them rest by your side. Face your feet forward about shoulder width apart. Bend your knees slightly . . . just a tiny bit. Good. Now rest your hands by your sides and circle your shoulders a few times. Let your shoulders drop down and relax. Shake your arms and hands. Let them relax. Good. Now focus on your breathing. Breathe in one long, slow breath. Breathe out slowly and think to yourself, "Relax." Breathe in slowly. Breathe out slowly . . . letting all the tension flow out of your body.

For the next five breaths, continue to breathe easily and slowly. Each time you breathe out, think to yourself, "Relax."

Good. You feel good. You feel great. You are relaxed. You are in control of yourself, your focus, and your body. You feel confident and happy to be alive. Stretch your arms out to the side, bring them up over your head, and lower them back down to your sides. Feel the good energy flowing within your body. Relax. Focus on some good things you want to do and make the best of the rest of this great day.

## One-Breath Relaxation

One of our goals in teaching children, teens, and adults to relax themselves is to help them develop their ability to relax to the point that they are able to relax quickly (within the space of one or two breaths) whenever it may be helpful. Practicing One-Breath Relaxation is a great way to learn to do this.

Your goal in learning to relax is to get so good at relaxing yourself that you can relax quickly whenever you are tense, worried, upset, or simply want to feel completely relaxed or get a good night's sleep. You can learn to relax yourself quickly by practicing one-breath relaxation. Let's try it right now.

> Breathe in slowly—take in one long, slow, deep breath. As you breathe in, feel the air slowly filling your body.
>
> Breathe out slowly—let all the air and tension flow out of your body. As you breathe out, calmly say to yourself, "Relax," and feel the tension leave your body.
>
> Breathe in slowly—take in one long, slow, deep breath.
>
> Breathe out slowly—let all the air and tension flow out of your body.
>
> Let's try it one more time.
>
> Breathe in slowly—take in one long, slow, deep breath.
>
> Breathe out slowly—let all the air and tension flow out of your body.
>
> Relax.

Good. If you want to get really good at One-Breath Relaxation, every time you sit down, stand up, listen to someone, talk to someone, or do something active, do your One-Breath Relaxation. Every time you are in a stressful situation or something upsets you—at home, at school, when you are playing, in a game or competition, at work, or when you are with another person—try your One-Breath Relaxation. Simply take one long, slow, deep breath in, then slowly breathe out and think to yourself, "Relax."

Practice doing One-Breath Relaxation every day, whenever you want to focus better, learn something, perform better, or feel more relaxed. This will put you in control of your focus, your mind, your body, your tension, and your relaxation. See how good you can get at One-Breath Relaxation. See how many times you can use it today.

### Relaxing to music

Music is another great medium for relaxation with children, teens, and adults. They will respond very well by relaxing to music if you—or they—choose something they like or that they find very soothing. Music can elicit many different feelings, images, and emotions, some of which lead to excitement, others that lead to relaxation. Experiment with finding and helping participants find different kinds of music, tranquil sounds, or relaxing melodies that can help them relax readily and fully. Listening to the natural sounds in nature (on CDs or DVDs) can also be very relaxing.

## Clocking Heart Rate

Children, teens, and adults enjoy seeing and feeling how relaxation can slow down their heart rate. We often do this by taking their heart rate before and after relaxing. This is a great motivator to relax and an effective way for them to see and feel the effect that simple relaxation has on their bodies. There are simple heart rate monitors available that clip gently onto the earlobe and give a constant readout of heart rate. Children, youth, and adults love using them when they are doing relaxation activities and other focusing exercises. Any kind of a simple heart rate monitor that clips on easily is a very effective way of showing the immediate effects of tension and relaxation. There are also great heart rate monitors that can be strapped on the body, like a belt, which athletes often use, but they are much more expensive than the clip-on heart rate monitors.

If heart rate monitors are not an option for you or those with whom you live or work, do it the old-fashioned way. First, show them how to find their own pulse by gently placing the tips of their first two fingers on the underside of their wrist. If they stretch out all their fingers on one hand with their palm facing up, and look at their wrist, they will see two lines (tendons) just under the skin which are parallel to each other. Ask them to gently place two fingers on the thumb side of those tendons. There is a little dip there and that's where they will find their pulse. Some people prefer and find it easier to find their pulse in the front part of their neck, on either side of their neck. Find your own heart rate first and then help them find theirs. Let them experiment with finding their pulse in whatever way works best for them.

Before and after relaxation exercises, have the children take their own pulse rates for either thirty or sixty seconds. They can also work together with a partner where they count their partner's heart rate before and after one minute of relaxation. For some young children, counting and recording heart rates is in itself a good focusing exercise. Give them a signal to "**Start**" counting heart beats and then give them a signal to "**Stop**." Then let them write down the number of heart beats they counted.

## Reminders to Relax

Plan specific times for yourself to relax and respect that plan by actually relaxing at those times. Plan specific times to help others learn to relax and respect that plan by actually practicing relaxation activities at those times. This is an essential part of learning to live in more relaxed, balanced, and meaningful ways.

Choose, and help others choose, specific Relaxation Reminders (words, phrases, thoughts, or images) to relax. This is very important for relaxing in situations where you or others may feel overloaded, uncomfortable, worried, or stressed. Relaxation reminders might include: *Relax, Breathe, Calm, Connect, Focus, Follow your Breathing, Change Channels, Shift Focus, Click on the Relax or Flowing Stream Channel.* When first using Relaxation Reminders, repeat the reminder several times in a row. Relaxation Reminders can also be linked with your breathing, where you say the word "relax" or "calm" to yourself each time you breathe out.

Encourage participants to choose or create their own relaxation or focus reminders, and to use them whenever they want to relax or connect in more positive or relaxing ways. Help participants to practice and refine their relaxation reminders so they will work best when they need them most in any situation or context.

# Collaborative Learning

Children, teenagers, and adults can help each other learn to reduce stress and add relaxation, joy, and quality to their lives by sharing and discussing their personal experiences with stress and relaxation.

Begin by asking participants to share their responses to the following questions. This usually works best in small groups (not more than four or five people in a group).

## *Relaxing*

What kinds of things make you feel relaxed, happy, joyful, good about yourself, or good about others?

What does being relaxed feel like for you?

What do you think you can do every day to feel more relaxed and find more joy in your life?

What are your own **best ways** to relax and focus effectively?

## *Stressing*

What kinds of things make you feel stressed, uptight, tense, nervous, or worried?

What does being stressed feel like for you?

What do you think you can do every day to reduce the stress or worry in your life?

What are your own **best ways** to reduce stress and focus effectively?

When participants are working collaboratively in small groups, ask someone in each group to make a list of their collective best ways to relax and reduce stress. And ask group members how they think they can help each other to continue to improve their skills for relaxation and stress control.

Small or large group discussions aimed at enhancing people's lives can take place anywhere, in any context—in classrooms, teams, families, meetings, workshops, or partners interacting with one person at a time. Encourage all participants to share and discuss their own **best ways** to relax, reduce stress, find joy, and focus effectively. Ask for their ideas on how they can help each other (or other people such as friends, family members, teachers, teammates, or coaches) to improve their skills for relaxing, letting go of stress, and having a happier day—and a happier life.

## Live the Lessons You Are Learning

Continue to encourage your students, family members, and others who are important to you to *live* the Positive Living Skills they are learning (for example, Spaghetti Toes, Jelly Belly, One-Breath Relaxation, Flowing Stream, Tree It, Changing Channels, Focusing, Refocusing, or Treasure Hunting for Highlights). Challenge them to use these activities or others they may think of—every day. Then follow up with them by asking if they have tried anything to relax, focus, refocus, reduce stress, or add joy to their lives. Encourage yourself and people of all ages to keep using, practicing, and refining these activities. *Find an opportunity to try one of these relaxation or focusing activities every day. Share what you tried—and share what you learned from trying.* This way we will all continue to get better at learning, performing, relaxing, and living in positive and fully connected ways.

# 12

# Positive New Beginnings

*Positive Living Skills provide everyone with an opportunity for Positive New Beginnings.*

From the standpoint of everyday life . . . there is one thing we do know: that man is here for the sake of others—above all, for those upon whose smile and well-being our own happiness depends, and also for the countless unknown souls with whose fate we are connected by a word of sympathy. Many times a day I realize how much of my own outer and inner life is built upon the labors of my fellow men, both living and dead, and how earnestly I must exert myself in order to give in return as much as I have received.

—*Albert Einstein*

# Positive Beginnings Start Now

We are ending this book where we began—with the goal of creating the conditions for nurturing better children, better people, better learners, better performers, and a better world. To turn this global goal into a positive reality, we need people like you who care enough to begin acting on their positive intentions. Positive, real-world change begins to take root and grow when small groups of dedicated people begin to act on their good intentions—one person, one child, one class, one community—one step at a time.

The best time to begin teaching Positive Living Skills to people of all ages is NOW. The best place to start is with children and youth—while they are open and receptive and have most of their lives in front of them—to live, love, learn, perform, relax, focus, and contribute in positive ways. We all gain from learning to relax and focus in positive and connected ways. We all win by enhancing the quality of our personal interactions, embracing positive learning and performance opportunities, and raising the overall quality of our lives. Let's begin working together now to help more people become positive, respectful, and joyful human beings. Let's begin moving humanity forward right *now*.

One child, student, family member, teacher, coach, teammate, friend, or colleague who really cares about another person can make a huge positive difference in his or her life. One person who does something positive to help you or someone else in some small or big way—without wanting or expecting anything in return—can have a huge positive influence on your life and on the lives of others.

# Living in Positive and Caring Ways

One of the greatest gifts we can bestow upon other people (young and old) is to be Nice on their Feelings. There are millions of good people on our planet who enhance the lives of others every day, simply by being nice on their feelings. There are also many *destructive* people in communities and societies around the world who inflict harm on other people every day—physically, mentally, emotionally, spiritually, and financially.

People who are negative or destructive toward others usually have no empathy or compassion for others. They can do horrible or humiliating things to other people—and feel nothing. We have to be able to "feel" something in order to feel or care about someone else's feelings. Otherwise, hurting or destroying another person emotionally or physically is like slapping a mosquito or stepping on an ant: it doesn't matter and there is no emotion connected to it.

This is one of the reasons that nurturing empathy in all people and all cultures—at early ages—is so essential to our local and global humanity. Nurturing empathy needs to become a major humanitarian goal that is modeled and taught in all families, communities, preschools, elementary and secondary schools, and universities around the world.

Sadly, in many societies, there are people who grow to not care about anyone or anything but themselves. They don't "feel" any remorse about bullying, hurting, cheating, stealing, addicting, destroying, maiming, or even killing innocent or helpless people. People who grow to live with no compassion, no empathetic feelings, and no sense of regret for destructive, degrading, or inhumane acts become the real enemies of themselves and humanity. Uncaring, unfeeling people are at the root of many subcultures and societies that contribute to a distorted, violent, or inhumane world. This is one solid reason to begin teaching Positive Living Skills to all children in all corners of the world.

## Feeling Feelings

Our relationships and our world will immediately become a better place by beginning to nurture everyone's capacity to sense other people's feelings—to feel what other people are feeling, empathize with what others are feeling and care about other people's feelings. This is a critical skill for minimizing abuse and nurturing better people, better communities, and a better world for everyone.

When children or youth witness or participate in an inconsiderate or disrespectful act, ask them: "How would you feel if you were this person being mistreated in this way?" Help them try to imagine and "feel" what they might feel or others might feel in a similar situation. This will help them begin to develop and share their empathy skills—skills for jumping inside another person's feelings.

Children who are taught to respect and care about other people's feelings, rights, and personal boundaries at an early age learn to care about other people and their feelings. They are much less likely to intentionally inflict harm on other children, family members, or innocent people. Every child has the potential to grow in positive and caring ways, contribute to respectful, meaningful relationships, and be a part of building better communities, societies, and a better world. Learning Positive Living Skills will help children and youth around the world move along this positive path.

## Nice on My Feelings

People in all cultures will live more harmonious, relaxed, and joyful lives if they are simply nicer on each other's feelings. The following audio track introduces children and youth to some ways in which they can be more caring and supportive human beings. You can read this script to your children or let them listen to it on CD1 ("Spaghetti Toes"—"Nice on My Feelings"). After the children listen to the "Nice on My Feelings" story, ask them each to share at least one way they can be Nice on other people's Feelings. Write their positive suggestions down and post them in a place where everyone can clearly see them. Make it a goal for everyone to be Nice on other people's Feelings—every day.

Get yourself into a comfortable position.
Close your eyes.
Be very quiet and just listen to my voice.
Breathe in slowly. Breathe out slowly.
Breathe in slowly. Breathe out slowly.

Let yourself relax.

Continue to breathe easily and slowly while I tell you a little story about feelings. Listen very closely.

Feelings are probably the most important thing in the world.

One of the most important things you can do each day is be nice on other people's feelings, and one of the most important things other people can do is be nice on your feelings.

When you are nice on people's feelings, you make them feel good and you also make yourself feel good.

One of the worst things that people can do is hurt other people's feelings. Nobody likes people who are mean or nasty or who hurt other people.

One way kids hurt other kids is by hitting, pushing, kicking, punching, or fighting—which is not a nice thing to do.

But there is also another kind of hurt—and that is when someone hurts your feelings.

Kids can hurt your feelings when they are mean to you, say bad things to you, call you names, yell at you, laugh at you, make fun of you, tease you, say you are stupid or no good, or tell you you can't play with them or their friends. Those kinds of things hurt our feelings and make us feel bad, sad, or lonely inside.

Think about your own feelings. Think about what other kids do that hurts your feelings or makes you feel bad.

Think about how you feel when someone is mean to you, or pushes you, or yells at you, or calls you stupid, or won't let you play, or makes you feel left out or sad or bad.

If everyone does more things that make other kids feel good, and less things that make them feel bad, everyone will like each other more and everyone will be a lot happier. That would make everyone feel better.

How can YOU be nice on other kids' feelings?

Think about what other kids do that make you feel

good and do some of those things.

Do something or say something that will make them feel good or happy or important.

Say hello to them, smile at them, talk with them, ask them about the things they like to do, tell them about things you like to do, ask them to play with you or your friends, or play with them.

To make other kids feel good, just be nice on their feelings and make sure that you don't do things or say things that hurt them or make them feel sad or bad.

How can you help other kids be nice on your feelings?

First, be nice on *their* feelings.

Second, when someone is nice on your feelings, say, "Thank you, that made me feel really good."

Third, when someone is not nice on your feelings or your friends' feelings, say to them, "That wasn't very nice on my feelings, or my friends' feelings. That made me feel really bad. It would be a lot nicer, and people would like you a lot more, if you were nice on their feelings instead of hurting their feelings."

By thanking people when they are nice and telling them when they are not nice, you might help them learn to be nicer on other kids' feelings.

**Remember**: how good you feel when someone is nice on your feelings.

**Remember**: Every day you have lots of chances to make other people feel good—in school, at recess, at home, or wherever you are.

**Remember**: If you are nice on other people's feelings and they are nice on your feelings, everyone is happier.

## Nurturing Empathy

The **Nice on My Feelings** story you just read was written to get children thinking and talking about feelings—their feelings and other people's feelings. It was designed to begin building empathy skills and a sense of caring about other people and how they are feeling. The more children, teenagers, and adults learn to respect and care about other people's feelings and other people's lives—in all cultures—the better everyone's lives and the safer our world will be. Remind children that adults, family members, friends, teachers, coaches, and people they do not know have feelings, too. Also remind parents, teachers, and coaches that children have feelings, too—feelings that can easily be hurt or damaged, or easily nourished in positive ways every day.

The extent to which a person is capable of genuine empathy for another person is the best predictor for how that person will respect and respond to other people throughout her or his life. The most destructive people on our planet have one thing in common: a complete absence of empathy for other human beings. Nurturing empathy, genuine caring, cooperation, and positive collaboration with others is the best way to stop the tide of abuse and violence directed at others and our natural world. Empathy creates the foundation for compassion, love, harmony, reduced stress, more relaxation, and higher levels of humanity.

Empathy is grounded in feelings: feeling what you are feeling, feeling what others are feeling, sharing feelings, respecting feelings, and caring about other people's feelings. Empathy is a skill that allows human beings to *feel* another person's perspective on an emotional level and really care about what happens to her or him.

## Action steps to build empathy in children and youth

We can seize many opportunities to build empathy in children and youth. Here are a few ways to get started:

- Respond positively to children's early gestures of giving, caring, and sharing.

- Encourage cooperative, inclusive play where everyone is included and having fun (see **Cooperative Games** book in Resource section for examples).

- Use children's books, stories, or movies to discuss how different characters are feeling and how people could be nicer on each other's feelings. It is clear that many children feel an emotional connection to many storybook characters in books and movies. During or just after reading books or watching movies, ask the children what they were feeling during specific parts of the story. Ask them how they feel the character in the story was feeling. Share your own feelings as well. Let them know it is good to feel their feelings and feel other people's feelings—it makes us more human.

- Set up different role-play situations ("make-believe" or pretend-play scenarios) where children and youth act out being helpful, kind, considerate, and caring toward other people (young and older).

- Praise children and youth when they act in caring or sharing ways, when they take good care of younger children, pets, or animals, respect older people, or interact with our natural environment in respectful ways.

- Find or help children and youth find positive role models who are empathetic toward others and respectful of their feelings.

- Create or ask others to create positive role models for children and youth for TV or other sources of entertainment who exemplify caring and empathy toward others.

- Ask children, youth, and adults to share how they feel in different situations—for example, when they feel included or excluded, respected or not respected, valued or not valued.

- Discuss with children, students, friends, classmates, and colleagues how we can all be nicer or more respectful of all people's feelings.

- Remind children and youth that adults have feelings, too—family members, teachers, coaches—and to do their best to be nice on their feelings.

- Let your children or students see and feel your empathy for others. Talk about how you feel on the inside when someone is nice or not nice on your feelings. Share why you feel it is important to not intentionally hurt another person or another person's feelings.

- Be the best example you can of sharing, caring, and understanding other people's feelings.

The earlier and *more often* we nurture empathy in children and youth, the better our lives and our world will be.

For hundreds of additional simple activities and practical ideas for nurturing empathy, cooperation, confidence, and positive living for children and youth, see *Nice on My Feelings: Nurturing the Best in Children and Parents* and *Feeling Great: Teaching Children to Excel at Living* in the Resource section.

# Build More Positive Words and Ways

Encourage children, teens, and adults to use a more positive vocabulary; positive words followed by positive actions will make children and others feel valued, competent, appreciated, and accepted. Many people who have grown in negative ways do not have a vocabulary of positive words or actions to express good thoughts, appreciation, or positive feelings toward others. They also lack effective ways for being positive with themselves.

One way to create more positive words and ways is to ask small groups of children, teens, or adults to work together to create a list of positive or uplifting words, phrases, and actions that they can use with themselves (to feel good or enhance their own confidence) and to use with others (to make others feel valued, good, supported, confident, and appreciated). Ask participants in each group to:

1. Make a list of anything they can say, think, or do to make themselves feel good, valued, strong, positive, competent, confident, focused, or happy (at home, school, when playing games or sports, performing, dancing, singing, acting, working, in daily interactions, or in any context). For example: "I am good / I am strong / I can do this / I can learn this / I am competent / I have lots of good

qualities / I am a good person / I like the good parts of myself / if I decide to do something well or to help someone else, I can do it."

2.  Make a list of anything they can say or do to make *other people* feel good, valued, strong, positive, competent, confident, focused, or happy (at home, school, when playing games or sports, performing, dancing, singing, acting, working, in daily interactions, or in any context). For example: "You are a good person / you are strong / you can do this / you can learn this / you are competent / you have lots of good qualities / you are a good friend / I like you / I appreciate you / if you decide to do something well or to help someone else, you can do it."

## *Turn negative words or thoughts into positives*

When I ask children and youth to write down positive and negative things they say to themselves and others, they can often fill a whole page or chalkboard with negative words or phrases and only a few lines with positive words or thoughts. I ask them to look at each negative word, phrase, or thought and write down (or tell me) what the opposite would be. For example: "I am stupid" becomes "I am smart"; "I can't do this" becomes "I can do this"; "I will probably fail or mess up" becomes "I will succeed"; "I am no good" becomes "I am good at lots of things"; "we can't do this" becomes "we can do this, we can succeed, we can do anything if we decide to do it and focus on doing it." I challenge them to continue to find positives to replace anything negative that they say to themselves or others—and to see how often they can use those new positive words or phrases to be more positive with themselves and others.

# Create More Positive Role Models

Many movies, computer games, music videos, and television and Internet programs that are watched or played by children and youth glorify violence, create or reinforce a negative vocabulary, and provide inconsiderate or destructive role models. This creates an obstacle for many children and youth with respect to learning to live in more positive and respectful ways. Children and youth will benefit greatly from more positive role models—in the media and in real life—where caring and considerate people are highly valued and act and interact in positive ways. We desperately need to find ways to replace negative role models. This will support our children and youth on their journey toward living in a better and more positive world for all people.

## Create More Positive Opportunities to Simply Relax and Connect with Others

Children, teenagers, and adults who feel relaxed (not stressed), valued (not devalued), accepted (not rejected), and safe and secure (not threatened) are much more likely to become the positive people they have the potential to become. They are also more likely to ask meaningful questions, share their real concerns, and continue to develop positive human values. Positive communication that goes beyond the surface (in any context) is greatly enhanced when people share quiet time together, feel respected and relaxed, show respect toward each other, are free from outside distractions or interruptions, and connect fully with listening to each other. This does not happen often enough in our daily lives as children, teenagers, or adults.

## Create Positive and Supportive Environments

We can reduce a great deal of stress and negativity and add an abundance of joy to many lives simply by creating more positive, relaxed, and supportive environments in which to live, learn, play, work, perform, and interact.

# Don't Underestimate People's Capacity

Many children, youth, and adults who have been labeled as deficient, lesser people, or "stupid" have come to view themselves as incompetent or of lesser value—when they actually have a great deal to offer. Many people who might not learn as quickly, remember as clearly, speak as eloquently, or perform as well as others simply have not had an opportunity to learn and develop positive focusing skills. There is always a possibility for improvement, no matter where people start, how others "see" them, or how they "see" themselves. It is never too early or too late to learn (or teach others) to focus and live in more positive and respectful ways.

# Planting Seeds of Humanity

We certainly have the human capacity to create a better world for all people.

If we teach all children, teenagers, and adults to respect themselves—and the lives, feelings, and dreams of all people, in all communities and cultures—our world will become a better, safer, and more vibrant place for everyone.

## WE CAN HELP PEOPLE OF ALL AGES TO:

**Focus in Positive and Connected Ways**

**Strengthen their Wheel of Highlights**

**Strengthen their Pillars of Focus**

**Respect, value, and embrace the good parts of themselves and their capabilities**

**Respect, value, and embrace the good parts of others and their capacity to contribute**

**Relax and reduce unnecessary stress in their lives**

**Build a sense of empathy within themselves and others**

**Care about others and support them on their positive journeys**

My hope and dream is that from the humble seeds that have been planted in this book, combined with the positive initiatives that are already started in many parts of the world, a forest or ocean of new humanity will begin to grow. We are planting little positive seeds that have the potential to grow into something amazing. Every seed we plant may not become part of a strong and healthy forest or ocean of humanity that stretches around the world. However, many positive seeds will take root and grow. Our success will depend on how many seeds we plant, who is planting the positive seeds, how fertile the soil is, and how many of us choose to continue to nurture the seeds of positive living around the world.

Walking or running along this path will lead us to a better and more humane world for all people. The more caring people we can get to walk or run along this path, the better and more humane our world will become.

## A Footprint in the Sand; or Seeds for a New Humanity

At times, while I was engaged in writing this book, I stopped and reflected on my path in life and my journey with Positive Living Skills. I wondered if what I am doing and writing will be like leaving a footprint in the sand that will be washed away with the next wave or gust of wind; or if I am planting positive seeds for the beginning of a new reality. My dream is that it will lead to something that lives and grows within you and the minds and hearts of many other people—something that will stay with you, grow with you, and will be passed on to new generations.

A footprint in the sand versus planting positive seeds that take root and grow will be largely dependent on what YOU, and other people like you, do. When you put this book down on your table, desk, or bookshelf, will you act on something that you feel can be of value? Or will you just think that it's a good idea or bad idea and do nothing with it? The honest answer to this question will dictate what happens or does not happen in people's lives, families, schools, places of work and performance, communities, countries, and our future world.

You and I have an opportunity right here, right now, to DO SOMETHING POSITIVE that can really make a difference in many people's lives—and in our own lives. We just have to act on implementing and sharing what we already know. Pick your spots. Where do you want to leave your footprints, mind prints, or positive seeds for a better world?

## THE TIME IS NOW

**The time to begin building a more positive YOU is now.**

**The time to begin building more positive relationships is now.**

**The time to begin teaching children and youth to focus in more positive ways is now.**

**The time to begin building a more positive world is now.**

If WE do not seize this opportunity, this moment, to teach ourselves and others to focus in more positive and connected ways, who is going to do it?

- Focus on **Why You Can** and **How You Will** do the good things you want to do.

- Focus on making your time with yourself positive and your time with others count.

- Focus on walking, or running, along a path to more positive living.

- Focus on helping others to walk or run along a path to more positive living.

This will lead us all to a better and more humane world for all people.

There is nothing more powerful in your life than the power of a persistent, positive, and connected focus. There is nothing more powerful in our world than the collective power of a small group of dedicated people, or billions of people with a persistent, positive, and connected focus.

There are no hidden agendas in the pursuit of better people and a better world. We are not seeking personal, political, or financial gains, power, recognition, or control over other people or their resources. Our only goal is to help people of all cultures, beliefs, races, and ages to become better, more connected, harmonious human beings. This noble goal is within our stretched human potential.

If YOU genuinely care about people, want to contribute to others in positive and meaningful ways, and feel good about being nice on other people's feelings, you can help this Positive Living Skills initiative move forward—one small step at a time. I hope you are or will become one of these positive people, committed to positive, meaningful action.

## *IF NOT NOW—WHEN?*
## *IF NOT YOU—WHO?*

# RESOURCES
## CDs and Books by Terry Orlick

## Compact Discs

All of the following CDs are available at *www.gsph.com* (the General Store Publishing House Web site).

## Positive Living Skills Audio CDs for Children, Tweens, Teens, and Adults

CD 1 *Spaghetti Toes*—Positive Living Skills for Children and Youth

CD 2 *Changing Channels*—Positive Living Skills for Children and Youth

CD 3 *Focusing through Distractions*—Positive Living Skills for Children, Youth, and Adults

CD 4 *Relaxation and Joyful Living*—Positive Living Skills for Children, Youth, and Adults

## Zone of Excellence Audio CDs for Athletes and Performers in Any Field

CD 1 *Focusing for Excellence—Relaxation and Stress Control Activities*

CD 2 *Focusing for Excellence—Exercises for Strengthening Focus and Performance*

CD 3 *Focusing for Excellence—Practicing in the Zone*

CD 4 *Focusing for Excellence—Performing in the Zone*

## Books

Halliwell, W., T. Orlick, K. Ravizza, and T. Rotella. *Consultant's Guide to Excellence*, 2003. Available from *www.gsph.com*

Orlick, T. *Coaches' Guide to Psyching for Sport*. Champaign, Ill.: Human Kinetics Publishers, 1986.

———. *Cooperative Games and Sports: Joyful Activities for Everyone.*

2nd ed. Champaign, Ill.: Human Kinetics Publishers, 2006.

———. *The Cooperative Sports and Games Book*. New York, N.Y.: Pantheon Books, 1978.

———. *Embracing Your Potential: Steps to Self-discovery, Balance and Success in Sports, Work and Life*. Champaign, Ill.: Human Kinetics Publishers, 1998.

———. "Enhancing Children's Sport and Life Experiences." In *Children and Youth in Sport,* edited by F. Smoll and R. Smith, 179–221. Dubuque, Iowa: Kendall/Hunt Publishers, 2002.

———. *Feeling Great: Teaching Children to Excel at Living*. 3rd ed. Carp, Ont.: Creative Bound, 2004. Available from *www.gsph. com.*

———. *In Pursuit of Excellence* (Audio-book Edition). Champaign, Ill.: Human Kinetics Publishers, 1997.

———. *In Pursuit of Excellence: How to Win in Sport and Life through Mental Training*. 4th ed. Champaign, Ill.: Human Kinetics Publishers, 2008.

———. *Nice on My Feelings: Nurturing the Best in Children and Parents*. Carp, Ont.: Creative Bound, 1995. Available from *www.gsph.com.*

———. *Psyching for Sport: Mental Training for Athletes*. Champaign, Ill.: Human Kinetics Publishers, 1986.

———. *The Second Cooperative Sports and Games Book*. New York: Pantheon Books, 1982.

———. *Winning through Cooperation*. Washington, DC: Hawkens and Associates, 1978.

Orlick, T., and C. Botterill. *Every Kid Can Win*. Chicago: Nelson Hall Publishers, 1975.

Orlick, T., J. McNally, and T. O'Hara. "Cooperative Games: Systematic Analysis and Cooperative Impact." In *Essential Readings in Sport Psychology,* edited by D. Smith and M. Barr–Eli, 121–152. Champaign, Ill.: Human Kinetics, 2006.

Orlick, T., and J. Partington. *Psyched: Inner Views of Winning*. Ottawa, Ont.: Coaching Association of Canada, 1986. Available free on-line at *www.zoneofexcellence.ca.*

# Articles Available Free On-line at
## www.zoneofexcellence.ca—Journal of Excellence.

Amirault, K., and T. Orlick. *"Finding Balance within Excellence."* *Journal of Excellence* Issue 2.

Gilbert, J., and T. Orlick. *"Teaching Skills for Stress Control and Positive Thinking to Elementary School Children."* *Journal of Excellence* Issue 7.

Hester, K., and T. Orlick. *"The Impact of a Positive Living Skills Training Program on Children with Attention-Deficit Hyperactivity Disorder."* *Journal of Excellence* Issue 11.

Hjartarson, F. *"Lessons Learned*: Mental Training with Young Offenders and Children at Risk." *Journal of Excellence* Issue 4.

Julien, K. *"Mental Skills Training for Children and Young Athletes."* *Journal of Excellence* Issue 7.

Klingenberg, M., and T. Orlick. *"Teaching Positive Living Skills to a Family with Special Needs."* *Journal of Excellence* Issue 7.

Koudys, J., and T. Orlick. *"Coping with Cancer: Lessons from a Pediatric Cancer Patient and His Family."* *Journal of Excellence* Issue 7.

McMahon, S., S. Partridge, and T. Orlick. *"Positive Living Skills: Skating through Adversity."* *Journal of Excellence* Issue 12.

Orlick, T. *"Making the Impossible, Possible, within a Relationship: An Interview with Lisa and Mike."* *Journal of Excellence* Issue 9.

———. *"Nurturing Positive Living Skills for Children: Feeding the Heart and Soul of Humanity."* *Journal of Excellence* Issue 7.

Orlick, T., and C. Hadfield. *"Interview with Chris Hadfield,* Canadian Astronaut." *Journal of Excellence* Issue 2.

Orlick, T., and S. Partridge. *"Positive Living Skills for Teenagers: A Youth Intervention."* *Journal of Excellence* Issue 12.

Orlick, T., and C. Tribble. *"Interview with Curt Tribble,* Elite Surgeon." *Journal of Excellence* Issue 5.

Partington, J. *"Excellence through Collaboration."* *Journal of Excellence* Issue 5.

Taylor, S., and T. Orlick. *"An Analysis of a Children's Relaxation/ Stress Control Skills Program in an Alternative Elementary School*

Setting." *Journal of Excellence* Issue 9.

Theberge, N. *"Mental Skills Training with Children in a Summer Camp Context." Journal of Excellence* Issue 7.

Towaij, N., and T. Orlick. *"Quality of Life in the High Tech Sector:* Excellence in Work and Nonwork." *Journal of Excellence* Issue 3.

Zitzelsberger, L., and T. Orlick. *"Balanced Excellence:* Juggling Relationships and Demanding Careers." *Journal of Excellence* Issue 1.

# Related Articles in Traditional Journals

Gilbert, M., and T. Orlick. "Evaluation of a Life Skills Program with Grade Two Children." *Elementary School Guidance and Counseling Journal* 31 (1996): 139–51.

Orlick, T. "Cooperative Play Socialization among Preschool Children." *The Journal of Individual Psychology* 2 (1) (1981): 54-64.

———. "Enhancing Love and Life Mostly through Play and Games." *Journal of Humanistic Education and Development* 17 (4) (1983): 153–64.

———. "Positive Socialization via Cooperative Games." *Developmental Psychology* 17 (4) (1981): 426–29.

Orlick, T., Q. Zhou, and J. Partington. "Cooperation and Conflict among Chinese and Canadian Kindergarten Children." *Canadian Journal of Behavioural Science* 22 (1) (1990): 20–25.

St. Denis, M., and T. Orlick. "Positive Perspective Intervention with Fourth Grade Children." *Elementary School Guidance and Counseling Journal* 31 (1996): 52–63.

# About the Author

**T**erry Orlick has committed his life to fulfilling a dream of harmony and excellence where people of all ages and cultures are nurtured to become better people, better performers, and contributors to a better world. He has charted new paths to performance excellence and quality living through Positive Living Skills that are essential for attaining and sustaining the highest levels of joy and personal excellence. Positive Living Skills empower children, youth, and adults to lift the quality and joyfulness of their own lives and enhance the lives of others. In this book, Orlick provides detailed guidelines on how to implement Positive Living Skills to enhance the lives of children, youth, and adults throughout the world.

Dr. Orlick is a professor in the Faculty of Health Sciences, School of Human Kinetics, University of Ottawa, Canada, where he teaches and conducts research on performance excellence and quality living. He has degrees from Syracuse University, The College of William and Mary, and the University of Alberta and is founder and editor of the innovative, free, on-line *Journal of Excellence* (*www. zoneofexcellence.ca*). Dr. Orlick shares his ideas through writing, teaching, presentations, and applied workshops on quality living, performance excellence, and positive living, throughout the world.

GSPH

***ORDER MORE COPIES FROM***

**GENERAL STORE PUBLISHING HOUSE**
499 O'Brien Rd., Box 415, Renfrew, ON  K7V 4A6
1.613.432.7697 or 1.800.465.6072
Fax  1.613.432.7184 • www.gsph.com     VISA  MasterCard